The **ESSENTIALS**® of

Anthropology

D1117896

Michael V. Angrosino, Ph.D.
Professor, Department of Anthropology
University of South Florida, Tampa, Florida

Research & Education Association
Visit our website at
www.rea.com

Research & Education Association
61 Ethel Road West
Piscataway, New Jersey 08854
E-mail: info@rea.com

THE ESSENTIALS®
OF ANTHROPOLOGY

Published 2008

Printed in the United States of America

Library of Congress Control Number 2002106970

ISBN-13: 978-0-87891-722-8
ISBN-10: 0-87891-722-5

What REA's Essentials®
Will Do for You

This book is part of REA's celebrated *Essentials*® series of review and study guides, relied on by tens of thousands of students over the years for being complete yet concise.

Here you'll find a summary of the very material you're most likely to need for exams, not to mention homework— eliminating the need to read and review many pages of textbook and class notes.

This slim volume condenses the vast amount of detail characteristic of the subject matter and summarizes the **essentials** of the field. The book provides quick access to the important facts, principles, theories and practices in the field.

It will save you hours of study and preparation time.

This *Essentials*® book has been prepared by experts in the field and has been carefully reviewed to ensure its accuracy and maximum usefulness. We believe you'll find it a valuable, handy addition to your library.

Larry B. Kling
Chief Editor

CONTENTS

CHAPTER 1

INTRODUCTION

1.1 WHAT IS ANTHROPOLOGY?

Anthropology is the study of human behavior in all places and at all times. It combines humanistic, scientific, biological, historical, psychological and social views of human behavior. Anthropology is divided into two broad subfields:

Physical Anthropology is the study of the biological, physiological, anatomical and genetic characteristics of both ancient and modern human populations. Physical anthropologists study the evolutionary development of the human species by a comparative analysis of both fossil and living primates. They study the mechanics of evolutionary change through an analysis of genetic variation in human populations.

Cultural Anthropology is the study of learned behavior in human societies. Most cultural anthropologists specialize in one or two geographic areas. They may also specialize in selected aspects of culture (e.g., politics, medicine, religion) in the context of the larger social whole. Cultural anthropology is further subdivided as follows:

1) **Archaeology** is the study of the cultures of prehistoric peoples. It also includes the study of modern societies, but from the evidence of their material remains rather than from direct interviews with or observations of the people under study.

2) **Ethnography** is the systematic description of a human society, usually based on first-hand fieldwork. All generalizations about human behavior are based on the descriptive evidence of ethnography.

3) **Ethnology** is the interpretive explanation of human behavior, based on ethnography.

4) **Social Anthropology** is the study of human groups, with a particular emphasis on social structure (social relations, family dynamics, social control mechanisms, economic exchange).

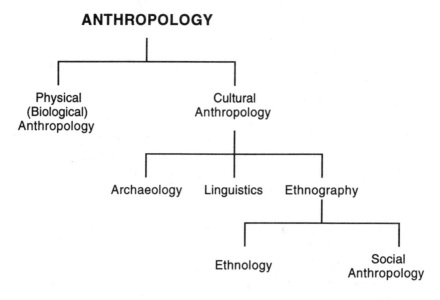

FIGURE 1.1 — The Subfields of Anthropology

5) **Linguistics** is the study of how language works as a medium of communication among humans. Language is the vehicle through which all culture is learned and transmitted.

1.1.1 DEFINING CHARACTERISTICS OF ANTHROPOLOGY

Holism is the belief that the experiences of a human group are unified and patterned. No one aspect of human behavior can be understood in isolation from all the rest.

Culture is the organized sum of everything a people produces, does, and thinks about – all of which they learn as members of a particular social group. A people's culture develops over time as they adapt to their environment.

Comparative Method is the belief that generalizations about human behavior can only be made on the basis of data collected from the widest possible range of cultures, both contemporary and historical.

Relativism is the belief that we cannot make value judgments about a culture based on standards appropriate to another culture. When such judgments are made on the basis of one's own culturally derived values, it is said that we are making **ethnocentric** judgments.

Fieldwork is the study of cultures in their natural settings, the communities in which people live, work and interact on a regular basis.

Anthropologists attempt to live for an extended period of time among the people they study. They are both **participants** in and **observers** of the culture of the group.

1.2 THE DEVELOPMENT OF THE ANTHROPOLOGICAL PERSPECTIVE

Anthropology is a product of Western civilization, but one that was relatively late to develop. By and large the Greek and Roman philosophers were more concerned with speculations about ideal societies than with descriptions of living ones.

A comparative approach was inaugurated in the Renaissance, with the rediscovery of the past of Western civilization.

Study of contemporary non-Western people began in earnest with the European discovery of the Americas. Aside from the reports of travellers and missionaries, the Age of Exploration resulted in two works of real anthropological interest:

1) **Sahagun's** study of Aztec beliefs and customs.

2) **Lafitau's** study of the Iroquois and Huron of western New York State.

Scientific anthropology is based on several key assumptions:

1) Cultures evolve through time.

2) Peoples adapted to similar environments in distant parts of the world will establish roughly similar cultures.

3) Human behavior is shaped more by what we learn as members of a social group than by what we inherit genetically. There is no one interpretation or explanation of culture to which anthropologists subscribe. There are, however, several major orientations which guide the explanations of anthropologists.

Evolutionism is the belief that all cultures develop in a uniform and progressive manner. All societies pass through the same stages of development and reach a common end, since the basic problems which all humans have to face are fundamentally similar. This orientation, which is also known as **unilineal evolutionism**, flourished in the late 19th century. Key figures: Edward B. Tylor and Lewis Henry Morgan.

Diffusionism is the belief that cultures develop not so much by adapting themselves to specific environments as by borrowing traits from other people. This orientation flourished in the early 20th century. Key figures: G.E. Smith, Fritz Graebner and Clark Wissler.

Historical Particularism, which was founded on the objection to the evolutionist model, stresses the wide range of cultural variability. It is suspicious of "universal laws" of human development and advocates the study of the particular historical development of specific societies as a necessary prerequisite to the formulation of generalizations about cultural evolution. This orientation was founded by Franz Boas early in the 20th century, and dominated anthropology in the United States until the 1960s.

Functionalism, which was another reaction to the extremes of evolutionism, is based on the analysis of specific traits of culture and the ways in which they serve the needs of individuals within the society. This orientation is associated with Bronislaw Malinowski who influenced anthropology in Britain from the period of World War I through the 1940s.

Structure-Functionalism, a variant of Malinowski's functionalism, advocated the analysis of specific traits and the ways in which they serve to maintain the equilibrium of the social structure (rather than the needs of the individuals). This point of view is associated with A.R. Radcliffe-Brown, who was a contemporary of Malinowski.

Psychological Anthropology is an attempt to analyze the interaction of cultural and psychological variables in the development of both culture and individual personality. This approach was stimulated by the translation of Freud's work into English in the 1920s. Key figures: Edward Sapir, Margaret Mead, Ruth Benedict, Ralph Linton, Abram Kardiner and John Whiting.

Neo-evolutionism is the attempt to formulate scientifically testable propositions about cultural evolution, as distinct from the speculative generalizations of the early evolutionists.

Universal evolutionism (general evolutionism) is the concern with the dynamics of culture as a general phenomenon, rather than with specific change within particular cultures. Key figure: Leslie White (1930s-50s).

Multilineal evolutionism (specific evolutionism) is concerned with patterns of interaction of culture and environment. It is sometimes also known as "cultural ecology." Key figure: Julian Steward (1940s - present).

Structuralism is the analysis of culture as represented in expressions such as art, ritual and the patterns of daily life. These surface representations are reflections of underlying logical structures of the human mind. Key figure: Claude Levi-Strauss (contemporary).

Ethnoscience is the attempt to derive rules of culturally conditioned behavior by a detailed logical analysis of ethnographic data as seen strictly from the natives' point of view. Key figures: Ward Goodenough and Charles Frake (contemporary).

Sociobiology is the belief that human behavior, including social behavior, is basically the product of genetic and environmental influences. Key figures: Napoleon Chagnon and William Irons (contemporary).

CHAPTER 2

HUMAN EVOLUTION

2.1 GENETICS AND EVOLUTION

All organisms are groups of cells. Every cell is reproduced from other cells. The basic principles of **cellular reproduction** are as follows:

1) Every cell is the product of reproduction of a single pair of original sex cells (**gametes**); the male sex cell is the sperm, the female is the ovum. The fusion of the two gametes produces a zygote, a fertilized egg.

2) The egg grows by repeated division of its cells.

3) The division of a cell is known as **mitosis**. The cell first reproduces its genetic material, and then divides, so that each offspring cell contains exactly the same genetic material as the parent cell.

4) Sex cells do not reproduce their genetic material, and so when they divide (the process of **meiosis**), the offspring cells receive only one-half the genetic material.

5) Human cells contain 46 **chromosomes**, which are chains of **genes**. Genes are the units of heredity; they contain the chemical code which governs the production of the organism. Human sex cells contain 23 chromosomes.

Gregor Mendel (1822 – 1884) formulated the basic laws of genetic inheritance as a result of experiments with cultivated plants. The Mendelian Laws are as follows:

1) **Law of Segregation** – Genes never blend, but behave as independent units; they pass intact from one generation to the next, and may or may not produce visible traits in every generation.

2) **Law of Independent Assortment** – The genes governing a given trait are independently assorted among offspring and are expressed independently of the location of other genes on the chromosome.

3) **Law of Lineal Order of Genes** – The genes for specific traits are located in regular sequence along a chromosome and are linked by chemical bonds so that they are normally inherited as a group.

In sexual reproduction, each individual receives two matching pairs of genes of each type – one from each parent. The genes that match up at the same chromosome site are **alleles** for that trait.

The total range of genes transmitted to a zygote is its **genotype**. If the pair of alleles for a trait is the same, the zygote is **homozygous**, and the organism will show whatever trait is expressed in that identical pair. But if the alleles are unlike, the zygote is **heterozygous**; the trait expressed will depend on which of the pair is **dominant** and which is **recessive**. The observable physical characteristics of an organism are known as its **phenotype**.

A **Mendelian population** is a localized group of members of a species who interbreed and occasionally breed with members of other populations of the same species. All the genes possessed by this population make up its **gene pool**.

The **Hardy-Weinberg Law** states that if mating within a population of infinite size is random, and if **mutations** (alterations in the genetic code, such that the phenotypic expression of a trait is changed) do not occur, then the frequencies of genes in the gene pool will remain constant over generations. But this equilibrium is not possible in real circumstances, so the frequencies of genes change often over time.

Evolution is successive change in the gene frequencies of populations. Evolutionary processes (i.e., factors that upset the genetic equilibrium) are as follows:

1) **Mutation** – (explained above).

2) **Natural selection** – Within a population, the individuals that reproduce most are the best adapted to their environment, and they therefore contribute a progressively larger proportion of descendants to the population; as their genes become preponderant in the population, the gene pool will be altered. Evolution has occurred. The principle of natural selection was the most important contribution of **Charles Darwin** (whose *On the Origin of Species* was published in 1859) to evolutionary theory.

3) **Population mixture (gene flow)** – This is the interbreeding between two populations with different gene pools, resulting in alterations in both pools.

4) **Gene drift** – This is the loss of material from the gene pool in a small population that interbreeds over many generations.

Evolution is not headed anywhere in particular; it is a **random** process of **gradual** adaptation of populations to their changing environments. Sometimes change results in **extinction**, the failure of a population to adapt to environmental change.

2.2 HUMAN VARIATION

All living humans belong to a single genus and species, **Homo sapiens**. But this species is divided into subgroups, based on different frequencies of alleles for various physical traits.

The old notion of **race**, which was often seen as a fixed and bounded population, has been supplanted by the concept of **clinal variation**. Anthropologists now speak about gradients or geographic distributions of specific variant traits, rather than about fixed races. The basic principles of clinal studies are as follows:

1) **Gloger's Rule** — Mammals and birds inhabiting warm and humid areas have darker skin pigmentation than those of the same species in cooler, drier areas; especially dry areas are marked by populations with yellow and/or reddish-brown pigmentation.

2) **Bergmann's Rule** — Overall body size within the same species decreases in warmer areas, increases in cooler areas.

3) **Allen's Rule** — The size of protruding body parts (e.g., tails, ears, bills) within the same species is reduced in

11

cooler areas and increased in warmer areas.

A **geographic race** is a localized population that has historically interbred more within itself than with outsiders. There may be physical barriers to interbreeding (e.g., mountains, seas). Traits that are particularly adaptive in a given area will be most frequent in populations historically localized in that area.

There is no scientifically documented relationship between race and intelligence. The capacity to learn is independent of the biological factors associated with the distribution of physical traits.

2.3   THE LIVING PRIMATES

All living things are classified according to a system (**taxonomy**) developed by the naturalist **Linnaeus** in the mid-18th century. The taxonomy is based on progressively more specifically inclusive groups. The classification implies common ancestry as well as physical resemblance. The major categories in the taxonomy are Kingdom, Phylum, Subphylum, Class, Subclass, Infraclass, Order, Family, Genus, Species and Variety. Humans belong to the **Animal** kingdom, of the **Chordate** phylum (presence of a spinal cord and nervous system), of the **Vertebrate** subphylum (presence of bony skeletal structure), of the **Mammal** class (nursing of young by female mammary glands), of the **Eutheria** subclass (live births), of the **Placental** infraclass (fetus nourished directly through mother's bloodstream).

Humans are members of the **Primate** order and demonstrate these characteristics:

1)   increased size and complexity of brain;

2) eyes located forward on skull; eye socket protected by bony ride; overlapping fields of vision (depth perception: stereoscopic vision):

3) reduced snout and jaws; lessened sense of smell;

4) **prehensile** hands (i.e., capable of grasping); five digits on hand; nails rather than claws; digits rich in nerve sensors;

5) increased hand-eye coordination;

6) five digits on feet;

7) postnatal development of offspring is prolonged; and

8) fewer, smaller, more efficient teeth doing more different kinds of tasks.

Other than humans, most living primates are **arboreal** (adapted for life in or near trees) and **tropical** in distribution. The living primates are as follows:

1) **Prosimians** (e.g., tree shrew, tarsiers, lemurs, lorises) – oldest primate type; survive only in marginal areas; resemble rodents and insectivores; primarily **nocturnal** (active at night).

2) **Anthropoids,** including **Platyrrhines** (New World monkeys) – flat faces, long and usually prehensile tails; and **Catarrhines**, including:

Cercopithecoids (Old World monkeys, e.g., macaques, langurs, baboons, and other monkeys of Africa and Asia) – quadrupeds (can walk on all fours) and lack the prehensile tail.

Hominoids — a) **Hylobatids** (gibbons and siamangs; Asia); arboreal, generally small in body size; b) **Pongids** (the "great apes" — chimpanzees and gorillas of Africa, orangutans of Asia); semi-erect posture, tailless; c) **Hominids** (living humans and their extinct direct ancestors). Humans are not "descended from" apes; rather humans and apes are descended from a common ancestor.

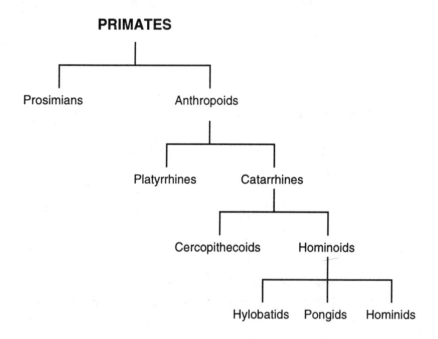

FIGURE 2.1 — The Primate Order

Primate social behavior manifests itself as follows:

1) multigenerational social groups with year-round association of the sexes;

2) prolonged infant dependency and protection of females and young by the males;

14

3) incipient tool use and food sharing; and

4) communication without capacity for speech.

   Hominids build on these "proto-cultural" bases:

1) transition to hunting large game and eating meat;

2) fully upright posture and regular reliance on tool-making and tool use;

3) family groupings with local bands;

4) outgroup mating; and

5) speech.

CHAPTER 3

HUMAN DEVELOPMENT

3.1   THE STUDY OF FOSSIL PRIMATES

A **fossil** is any preserved remnant of a living creature. The most common fossils are shells, bones and imprinted molds. They may be found buried in the earth, or preserved in tar pits, logs, layers of permafrost (permanently frozen ground in polar regions), or in glaciers.

Paleontologists try to reconstruct extinct life forms from the fossil evidence. Anthropologists are particularly interested in fossil primates. They want to discover not only *what* our primate ancestors looked like, but the chronological sequence in which they developed.

There is no single common ancestor from which all the primates diverged. Primates have always had a diverse gene pool. Fossils are dated in two ways:

Relative Dating establishes only the sequential order of development. Some of the techniques of relative dating include the following:

1) **Palynology** – the analysis of pollen; establishes the climatic conditions in which a fossil lived by determining the

kinds of plants that flourished when that fossil was alive.

2) **Coprolitic analysis** – the analysis of fossilized fecal material; provides clues to what extinct life forms ate.

3) **Stratigraphy** – the analysis of geological deposits.

Fossils found in layers of earth can be dated relative to each other, as deeper layers had to have been formed earlier than those sitting on top of them.

Absolute Dating establishes the actual age of the fossil. The main techniques of absolute dating are as follows:

1) **Physiochemical Dating** measures the decay of certain radioactive isotopes. Since these elements decay (i.e., lose atoms and become non-radioactive) at a constant rate, it is possible to measure the age of an item by measuring the amount of radioactive decay it has undergone. The most familiar of these techniques measures the decay of radioactive **Carbon-14**, which is particularly important because it is found in organic materials, such as wood, bone and plant matter.

2) **Dendrochronology** measures the age of wood by an analysis of the growth of the rings of the parent tree; trees form rings of new material at a standard rate.

Geologic time begins with the formation of the first sediments 4-6 billion years ago. Major blocks of geologic time are known as **eras**. Major climatic and other environmental changes mark the transition from one era to the next.

Primates emerged during the **Cenozoic** era, the most recent geologic era. It began approximately 70 million years ago. The Cenozoic is subdivided into seven **epochs**: the Paleocene, Eocene, Oligocene, Miocene, Pliocene, Pleistocene and Holocene. Study of human ancestors focuses on the Miocene (began 25 million years ago), the Pliocene (began 13 million years ago) and the Pleistocene (began 5 million years ago).

The **Miocene** was marked by a mild, wet climate prevailing throughout the Old World. Such a climate stimulated the growth of forests, providing more ecological niches for the primates, which are basically **arboreal** in adaptation. Important fossil primates of the Miocene include the following:

1) **Dryopithecus** – a widespread genus, probably ancestral to the modern Great Apes;

2) **Pliopithecus** – probably ancestral to the modern Hylobatids.

The **Pliocene** was a period of drying, and hence of shrinking of the forests. Marginal primates not perfectly adapted to the forests either became extinct or were able to survive in non-forest environments. Such primates had certain characteristics that **pre-adapted** them to life on the ground. Such pre-adaptations included a reduction in the size of the canine teeth, with an increase in the size of the molars. These dental changes enabled the Pliocene primates to exploit more diverse food sources. Fossils of the genus **Ramapithecus** demonstrate this Pliocene shift to a ground-dwelling, seed- and small object-eating lifestyle.

The **Pleistocene** was an unstable epoch, during which cold and warm periods alternated. During periods of extreme cold, the polar icecaps expanded, and life forms either had to retreat to the relatively warmer tropics or become adapted to colder conditions. Primates, although basically tropical animals, began to adapt to non-tropical environments during the Pleistocene climate shifts.

There were four advances of the glacial ice during the Pleistocene. They are known in the Old World as the Günz, Mindel, Riss, and Würm glaciations, and in the New World as the Nebraskan, Kansasan, Illinoisan, and Wisconsonian glaciations. **Interglacial** periods separate the glacial advances.

50,000 years ago	Modern Geologic Time
100,000 years ago	4th Glacial (Würm, Wisconsonian)
200,000 years ago	3rd Interglacial
350,000 years ago	3rd Glacial (Riss, Illinoisan)
600,000 years ago	2nd Interglacial
750,000 years ago	2nd Glacial (Mindel, Kansasan)
1.5 million years ago	1st Interglacial
5 million years ago	1st Glacial (Günz, Nebraskan)

FIGURE 3.1 — The Pleistocene

3.2   THE FIRST HOMINIDS

Fossil evidence from the Pliocene is relatively scant, although a dramatic discovery in 1999 of a complete skull, dated at 3.5 million years, added to the fossil record of the middle of that epoch. Unearthed by an international team led by **Meave Leakey**, the skull is believed to point to a new genus and species of early human, **Kenyanthropus platyops** (Flat-faced Man of Kenya), who is thought to have lived in East Africa between 3.5 and 3.2 million years ago. This find—in the Turkana District of northern Kenya—suggests that there were at least two species considered to be predecessors of modern humans in existence in East Africa between 3 and 3.5 million years ago.

By the end of the Pliocene, the **Australopithecines**, a form now generally acknowledged to be hominid, had emerged. They became well-established throughout the Old World during the Pleistocene.

The first Australopithecine fossil was discovered by **Raymond Dart** near **Taung** in South Africa in 1925. This fossil struck the scientific community of that era as "too primitive" to be a human ancestor, and it was not until the 1960s that the Australopithecines were acknowledged to be hominids.

The Taung fossil was that of a child. More detailed descriptions of the Australopithecine type were made possible by the discovery of adult fossils at **Sterkfontein, Makapansgat, Swartkrans** and **Kromdraai** in southern Africa.

Australopithecine fossils were later discovered in East Africa and in parts of Asia, but not in Europe. A major site for hominid fossils has been **Olduvai Gorge** in what is now Tanzania in eastern Africa. Olduvai has been associated with the work of **Louis, Mary** and **Richard Leakey**. A deep canyon cut by a now vanished river, Olduvai's layers of sediment are constantly being exposed by natural weathering processes, and they have yielded an enormous number of fossils, as the river's banks made a very desirable habitat in Pleistocene times.

The genus **Australopithecus** is divided into three species: **africanus, robustus** and **boisei**.

It is generally believed that A. africanus is the species with the closest affinities to Homo sapiens. The typical africanus stood $4 - 4^1/_2$ feet tall and weighed $50 - 90$ pounds. Africanus features of note include the following:

1) In proportion to its body size, the **brain** of A. africanus was larger than that of other primates.

2) The skull has a rounded cranial vault.

3) The skull was oriented to the spinal column in such a way as to suggest upright, rather than quadrupedal posture.

4) The shape of the mouth, teeth and jaw is more like that of humans than of apes. The mouth area seems adapted to a widely diverse diet.

5) The shape of the pelvis was modified so as to support a creature that could stand and move about in an upright position.

6) The foot is structurally similar to that of humans (i.e., built to support weight), rather than to that of apes (which is more like a hand).

A. robustus was bigger and more muscular than africanus, and had larger teeth and jaws associated with a more specialized vegetarian diet.

A. boisei was differentiated by its skull, which is characterized by very large teeth, a massively boned face, and a small brain. These features seem related to a diet demanding prolonged grinding and chewing.

All the Australopithecines lived in "open" (i.e., non-forested) country. The africanus species seems to have had the most diverse diet, and its exploitation of animal products as sources of food seems to be linked to its development of tools.

Tools are essentially modifications of naturally occurring objects that extend their users' capacity to cope with their environment. Many animals can use tools, but only humans have made them an essential element in their adaptive process. Upright posture freed the hands of the Australopithecines to use tools more consistently. Their primate trait of stereoscopic vision enabled them to coordinate hand and eye movements effectively.

The characteristic Australopithecine tool was a piece of stone with a cutting edge formed by removing flakes from the core. This "pebble" tool, as it was originally called, served to cut, dig and chop. It is now known as an **Oldowan** tool (named by Leakey after Olduvai Gorge), and because of its consistent association with the lifestyle of the Australopithecines, their adaptation is known as **Oldowan Culture**.

Tool-making began approximately 3 million years ago. (There is ongoing debate over the classification of the tool-makers. Some scientists prefer to distinguish them from other Australopithecines by calling them Homo habilis.) Stones, or "lithic" resources were most important for tool-making, and so we speak of the "Stone Age" or the "lithic period." The first part of the Stone Age is known as the **Paleolithic** (literally, Old Stone Age), and the first part of that period, represented by Oldowan culture, is known as the Lower Paleolithic.

Overall, the most important stone of the Stone Age was **flint**, which is not only very hard, but which has the capacity to fracture along predictable lines if struck at the proper angle and with the proper amount of pressure. Correct fracturing of a piece of flint leaves a sharp and durable cutting edge.

3.3   THE EMERGENCE OF GENUS HOMO

The status of Homo habilis, as noted above, is still being debated. The first fossil form that is indisputably a member of our own genus, Homo, is known as **Homo erectus**.

Homo erectus probably evolved from Australopithecines of the africanus species as they migrated beyond their African place of origin. Australopithecine forms survived in some parts of the Old World while other groups were changing in the direction of genus Homo. But by the time of the second inter-glacial, Australopithecines were extinct and were replaced by Homo erectus. The first Homo erectus was discovered in **Java** in 1891 by **Dubois**. Features of "Java man" include the following physical traits:

1) a flat, receding forehead sloping back from massive brow ridges,

2) upright posture,

3) powerful jaws, and

4) a large palate with the lower face protruding.

It has not been clearly established whether the Homo erectus of Java made stone or bone tools.

A second variety of Homo erectus was discovered in China in the 1920s. The original site of these finds was a cave called **Choukoutien**, not far from the city of Beijing. This form of Homo erectus is sometimes referred to as "Peking man," from the old spelling of the city's name. All the original Choukoutien fossils were lost during World War II, but fortunately casts had been sent to the U.S. before the war.

Compared with the Java form, the Peking erectus demonstrated these characteristics:

1) a considerably larger brain capacity,

2) the controlled use of fire (which enhanced their ability to live in caves and hence find shelter in a very cold environment, northern China being much closer to the glacial edge than Java),

3) an array of stone tools, and

4) a social organization that seemed to allow for some cooperation in the hunting of larger animals.

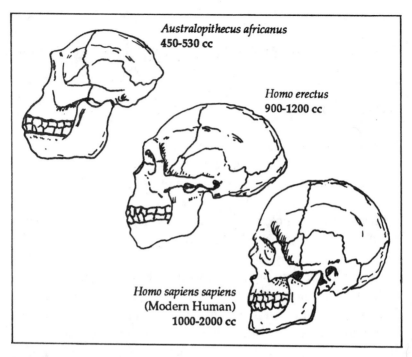

FIGURE 3.2 — Cranial Capacities in Hominid Evolution

The Peking form of Homo erectus was physically indistinguishable from modern Homo sapiens from the neck down. The significant site of human evolution for the past million years has thus been the skull and brain. Homo erectus in Peking apparently practiced cannibalism; they ate the brains and bone marrow of their fellows. But it is not known if people were killed specifically to be eaten, or if their parts were consumed after they had died of natural causes.

Homo erectus spread throughout the Old World by the time of the third glaciation. Their use of fire and more sophisticated tools enabled them to live in colder environments, as compared with the Australopithecines.

The tool tradition of most of the Homo erectus is known as

24

the **Acheulean**. It continued the Lower Paleolithic Oldowan culture. The most important tool was the "hand-axe," a core made from a piece of flint from which flakes had been removed, leaving a sharp point and at least two cutting edges. The hand-axe could be used for crushing, clubbing, and cutting. The flakes removed from the core were used for scraping hides, or for punching holes in hides, which could then be sewn into fitted clothing.

3.4 HOMO SAPIENS

Forms now classified as Homo sapiens appeared as early as the second interglacial. These finds were made at **Steinheim, Swanscombe** and **Fontechevade** in Europe. They are distinguished from contemporary Homo erectus forms by their expanded brain capacity.

Some of these Homo sapiens developed the flake-tool tradition known as the **Levalloisian**. Homo erectus flake tools were a by-product of the working of the core. Levalloisian flakes were made specifically, and were worked in finer, more careful detail. The most widely discussed of the early Homo sapien fossils was the **Neanderthal**, named after the site in Germany where it was discovered in 1856. Since this discovery took place before a comprehensive theory of evolution had been published, it immediately became the focus of great controversy.

Although the Neanderthal fossils looked "primitive," even "ape-like," to early observers, in fact these short, stocky, powerful, big-headed people were simply evidence of a highly specialized adaptation to the cold climate of Europe during the fourth glacial period.

Neanderthals are characterized by the following:

1) a large cranium,

2) large facial area,

3) short, massive spinal column,

4) short, heavy upper arm,

5) short forearm relative to upper arm,

6) massive, markedly curved thigh bone,

7) short shin bone, and

8) very short leg in proportion to thigh.

This "classic Neanderthal" type survived until approximately 40,000 years ago.

It is now known that Neanderthals were more widely dispersed, and more physically varied than originally suspected. The "classic" types were specifically adapted to the glacial cold, but other Neanderthals, living in warmer areas, do not exhibit such extreme adaptations.

Neanderthals were basically big-game hunters. Their tool tradition is known as the **Mousterian,** and was marked by increasing sophistication in the use of a variety of flakes, as well as core tools. The Neanderthals also used bone and probably wood to make tools. The Mousterian is characteristic of the **Middle Paleolithic** culture.

Neanderthals were cave dwellers, at least part of the time. Evidence of the Neanderthals' "humanness" is found in their practices:

1) burial of the dead, and

2) development of a ritual cult centered on the symbolic figure of the bear.

The Neanderthal-type was gradually replaced by modern-looking Homo sapiens by the end of the fourth glacial period. Physical features of modern Homo sapiens include the following:

1) the long bones of the leg are straighter, and more slender than those of the Neanderthals;

2) the arm is longer and less robust;

3) the brain case is rounded;

4) the face and lower jaw are reduced in size;

5) the brow ridges are much reduced; and

6) the molars are smaller and the teeth are set in an arch enclosing a smaller palate.

The cultures of these modern Homo sapiens were diverse, and they characterized the **Upper Paleolithic** period. In addition to greater elaboration of tool traditions, Upper Paleolithic culture was marked by the emergence of **art**, including painting (on the walls of caves), engraving, and sculpture.

It is assumed that Upper Paleolithic art had **magical** connotations; to draw a picture of a desired event (e.g., a large and fertile herd of animals to be hunted) was to influence that outcome.

Migration of humans to the Americas began with Upper

Paleolithic hunters following game across the land bridge across the **Bering Strait.** This migration began between 20 – 30,000 years ago. Until then, it must be remembered, there were no higher primates in the New World.

3.5 THE BEGINNINGS OF AGRICULTURE AND URBANISM

Hunting, which had sustained human beings and their hominid ancestors throughout the Paleolithic, became a less secure proposition as the environment changed following the retreat of the fourth glacier. The disappearance of the great "Ice Age" mammals forced people to find other means of support. Around 15,000 years ago, people began to settle in more or less permanent territories, and to turn to intensive **foraging** as a food-getting technique.

Ultimately, the collecting of wild plants and the hunting of small animals led to the domestication of plants and animals. The best known of the foraging culture was the **Natufian,** centered in the Middle East. This culture is part of the **Mesolithic,** or Middle Stone Age.

Domestication of plants and animals developed gradually – and probably in several different places independently – as responses to the need to insure a more steady food supply. Both Old and New World people were involved in this shift. Domestication may have begun with weeding and caring for wild patches of desired plants. It ultimately progressed to the deliberate planting of crops where and when they were needed.

Current evidence suggests that this process began in lightly forested upland grassy areas. It later moved into arid river valleys as the techniques of controlled irrigation were mastered. The development of agriculture marks the **Neolithic,** or New Stone Age. In addition to the domestication of plants and animals, the "Neolithic Revolution" included the following traits:

1) growth of permanent villages,

2) extension of trade,

3) development of pottery, basketry, weaving, and

4) the beginning of full-time specialized labor, since sufficient food could be produced by a farming class, freeing other members of the community to do other things, such as make tools, or engage in specialized ritual activities, or in trade.

In the irrigated river valleys, an intensively productive agrarian economy emerged, and by 5 – 7,000 years ago, cities were growing as centers of trade, government and ritual. These cities were ringed and supported by the farming villages. Major Old World valleys in which civilization flourished were the Tigris-Euphrates (Mesopotamia), the Nile (Egypt), the Indus (India), the Yellow (China) and the Mekong (Southeast Asia). In the New World agriculture and later civilization arose in the Valley of Mexico and in the valleys of the Andes in South America.

Civilization literally means the culture associated with the growth of cities. The main characteristics of civilization include the following aspects:

1) population growth and expansion,

2) centralized collection of agricultural surplus,

3) increased specialization of the labor force,

4) expanded trading networks,

5) monumental public works (temples, palaces, storehouses, irrigation systems),

6) highly developed art forms for aesthetic as well as practical purposes,

7) invention of writing to facilitate record-keeping,

8) invention of arithmetic, geometry and astronomy as means of keeping track of production and natural cycles,

9) growth of organized, centralized political leadership and the attendant expansion of the power of a ruling class, and

10) maintenance of power and expansion of influence through organized military action.

The Stone Age came to an end with the invention of metal technology. **Copper** was apparently the first metal to be used, probably for ornamental purposes. The discovery of the technology for combining copper and tin to form **bronze** ushered in the first of the Metal Ages. Bronze technology was difficult and expensive, and bronze was generally restricted to weapons and to items of wealth and prestige. The Bronze Age dates from approximately 3,000 years ago. The discovery of **iron** around 1,500 years ago, gave people access to a more plentiful material, allowing for the use of metals in more humble occupations.

With the spread of civilization and the development of literate, metal-based culture, subsequent developments in human chronology are generally treated by historians, rather than anthropologists. At this point, anthropologists turn from the question of what happened in pre-history, to the question of how culture works.

CHAPTER 4

HUMAN ADAPTATION TO THE ENVIRONMENT

4.1 ENVIRONMENT AND SUBSISTENCE: GETTING FOOD

Subsistence refers to the resources necessary to sustain life. Human beings are **omnivorous**: they are capable of eating both animal and plant matter. The ability of people to exploit these resources depends on the following:

1) what is available in the **physical environment** in which they live;

2) the size and density of their **population**, which determine the extent and character of needed resources; and

3) the technology available through their **culture** which will help them collect and make use of the resources.

Ecology is the study of the relationships between organisms and their environments. **Human ecology** is more specifically the study of how people relate to their environments, and

31

of the ways in which their activities influence both the natural and the social environments.

The natural environment does not cause people to behave in a certain way, but, by limiting the choices they can make, it is a very important factor in **determining** their culture. Deserts, the Arctic, high plateaus, and open grasslands all provide different resources, which restrict what people can do. Technology can certainly modify the environment, but only up to a point: irrigation can make farming possible in a desert, but no current technology will make the arctic tundra suitable for large-scale agriculture.

But within the limits imposed by the environment, the decisions made by people may vary considerably. For example, the desert Southwest of the U.S. has traditionally been occupied by two very different cultures — the agrarian **Pueblo** people, who live in settled villages, and the semi-nomadic **Navajo**, who are herdsmen. Pueblo culture is centrally organized, and is focused on rituals designed to promote social cohesion and control over natural phenomena. The Navajo did not traditionally have a centralized leadership and tended to emphasize the maintenance of personal autonomy. In effect, these people were responding to the same environment, but in very different cultural ways. The desert restricted the subsistence choices of both people, but did not absolutely force either of them into making particular decisions.

Typical subsistence strategies include the following:

Hunting/gathering – prevailed throughout the Paleolithic and survives among contemporary marginal tribal peoples. Typical hunting techniques include

1) assault (shooting, spearing, clubbing, axing, stabbing),

2) trapping and snaring,

3) the pitfall, and

4) poisoning.

The **atl-atl**, a device for lengthening the range of a thrown spear, and the **bow and arrow** were both invented during the Upper Paleolithic, and are among the most widely diffused hunting tools.

Some representative hunting/gathering people include the Cheyenne (Indians of the North American Great Plains) and the Eskimo.

Such societies were usually highly organized for the **communal** aspects of the hunt. Men usually hunted in teams. There was a sexual **division of labor**: men hunted, women gathered.

Intensive foraging – emerged during the Mesolithic, and survives among contemporary peoples living in environments of limited resources (such as deserts). Foragers depend on seeds, fruits and roots as the basics of the diet, as compared with gatherers, who use such resources only to supplement meat from the hunt. Foragers are necessarily semi-nomadic. They live in small bands because a fairly large territory must be exploited to provide enough food for the relatively few people. A typical foraging people are the Shoshone of the U.S. Great Basin.

Domestication – emerged during the Neolithic.

1) **Incipient agriculture** – growing crops in small garden plots by means of **digging sticks** or **hoes**.

2) **Intensive agriculture** – growing crops on large plots by means of **plows and draft animals**.

3) **Pastoralism** – reliance on flocks or herds of domesticated animals where the growing of crops is not feasible (mountains, deserts).

Deserts can only be made suitable for agriculture by irrigation, and open grasslands by plowing – both aspects of more advanced agricultural technology. Incipient agriculture therefore began in **lightly forested highlands**. Forests are cleared by **slash and burn** methods, which involve cutting down trees and burning the dead wood, exposing a light, weedless, humus-type soil. Such plots have to be left unplanted every few years so that the light soil can be replenished.

Some examples of incipient agricultural peoples include the following:

1) the Siang Dyak of Central Borneo (dry-rice cultivation on hilly slopes),

2) the Maya of Middle America (maize cultivation, known as the **milpa** system),

3) the Trobriand Islanders (yam cultivation in a tropical rain forest), and

4) the Indians of the Amazon (manioc cultivation).

Pastoral groups are organized for **transhumance,** the seasonal migration with flocks and herds. The typical movement is to upland summer ranges for grazing and then back to the lowlands in winter.

Pastoralists' animals are used as sources of hair/wool/hides, milk and dung (for fuel), and for load carrying and riding; they are rarely simply sources of meat for food. They are also the medium of exchange, and function something like money in a market economy.

4.2 ENVIRONMENT AND SUBSISTENCE: FINDING SHELTER

Technological adaptations in housing depend on these aspects:

1) the limitations imposed by the local environment (i.e., what sorts of building material are available? what extent of shelter is needed given the climate?); the most widely available materials for house-building are **wood** and **vegetable fiber**. In the Arctic, where wood is scarce, bone (whale ribs) has served to make poles for house frames. People in rainy areas roof their houses with thatch or bark. Such roofing is also good insulation. Houses in wet areas are often raised on stilts. Heavy mud or baked-clay roofs and walls are best suited to insulate houses in sunny, desert environments.

2) the subsistence pattern (farmers living in settled villages will have different housing needs from semi-nomadic foragers or pastoralists); foragers usually make do with a simple windscreen. Hunters and pastoralists live in tents, which are portable.

3) the social organization of the community (e.g., are there distinctions of wealth or social position to be marked by one's home?).

Some factors influencing housing and living patterns:

1) segregation of the sexes — in some societies, each woman

35

and her unmarried children live in their own houses, while men live communally in a clubhouse or men's house.

2) joint families — households shared by two or more nuclear families; the most famous example is the longhouse of the Iroquois of northern New York and southern Canada.

3) need for defense — the compact, walled pueblos were citadels protecting the peaceful farming people from their more warlike neighbors.

The **settlement pattern** of any community is described in terms of the spatial arrangement of people with relation to one another, to their resources, and to other societies. Types of settlement patterns are as follows:

1) nomadic (no permanent house site);

2) semi-nomadic (seasonal migration between established homesites;

3) compact, impermanent villages (typical of slash-and-burn gardeners, who must move every few years as soil is exhausted);

4) scattered neighborhoods (permanent, but dispersed sites associated with foraging people);

5) compact, permanent towns or villages; and

6) complex towns (trading centers) with outlying settlements.

	FOOD COLLECTORS	FOOD PRODUCERS		
	Hunters-gatherers	Horticulturalists	Pastoralists	Intensive Agriculturalists
Population density	Lowest	Low-moderate	Low	Highest
Maximum community size	Small	Small-moderate	Small	Large towns & cities
Nomadism/ permanence of settlements	Generally nomadic or seminomadic	More sedentary – communities may move after several years	Generally nomadic or seminomadic	Permanent communities
Food shortages	Infrequent	Infrequent	Frequent	Frequent
Trade	Minimal	Minimal	Very important	Very important
Full-time craft specialists	None	None or rare	Some craft specialists	High degree of craft specialization
Individual differences in wealth	Generally none	Generally minimal	Generally minimal	Yes, in land, animals & money
Political leadership	Informal	Some part-time political officials	Part- & full-time political officials	Many full-time political officials

Adapted and reprinted from Ember, Carol R. and Melvin Ember *Anthropology*, 5th ed. (1988), page 245. Reprinted by permission of Prentice Hall, Inc., Englewood Cliffs, New Jersey.

FIGURE 4.1 — Variation in Food-Getting: General Features of Recent Societies

4.3   TECHNOLOGY

Other manifestations of cultural adaptation to the environment include **tools** and **handicrafts**.

1) **Tools** are devices for transforming, transmitting or storing energy.

37

2) As subsistence techniques grow more efficient, more surplus is created, requiring containers for storage, equipment for cooking, utensils for eating and transport for trading.

3) Machines are tools for the conversion of one form of energy to another. Examples of machines known even to preliterate people include wedges, levers, rollers, bellows, looms and drills.

4) Materials used to make tools include the following:

   a) stone, either chipped (fashioned by striking off pieces), or polished (fashioned by abrading the surface)

   b) bone, shell, horn (serviceable, but less durable than stone)

   c) wood (its use probably dates from the Paleolithic, although it is not preserved, and so we cannot assess its origins, as we can for stone tools)

   d) metals (metallurgy requires sophisticated technical skills, although preliterate people in Africa and the New World had mastered that technology)

5) Handicrafts include the following:

   a) containers (made of skin, wood, clay)

   b) bags (flexible) and baskets (rigid): made of interwoven reeds, grass or shredded bark; baskets sealed with clay or pitch may be watertight

   c) pottery (a quicker, easier to make, and more efficient medium than basket weaving; initiated in Mesolithic times)

d) fabrics (weaving of fibers to produce a flexible cloth; worked on a loom to keep the fibers rigid while working)

e) felting (wetting, beating or compressing animal wools into a compact cloth)

f) bark cloth (use of bark fibers instead of hairs)

6) Clothing – used not only for protection of the body, but for ornamentation:

a) Different people have different standards of "modesty" — there is no universal standard for what a "well-dressed" person should wear.

b) Forms of ornamentation used by people with little or no clothing in the Western sense include: "G-strings," nose/ear/lip plugs, tattoos, scarification, face-painting, special hair-dos, and the blackening or knocking out or filing down teeth.

4.4   PROPERTY OWNERSHIP

Property may be defined as follows:

1) individual,

2) joint (belonging to a certain group, like a family), or

3) communal (belonging to the society as a whole).

Property may be fixed (real estate), or movable (chattel). It may be material, or incorporeal (e.g., an idea, a way of behaving, a social status, a magical charm).

It may be transferable (by gift, barter, sale, inheritance, confiscation), or inalienable (non-transferable).

It may be protected by civil law, supernatural sanctions, or customary usage.

Property is a social institution because it is both an object and the web of social relations establishing a limiting relationship between persons and that object.

The most important property is **land**, because society is usually territorially based, and because most subsistence is drawn from the soil. In non-Western societies, land is treated as a communal asset, although the right to **use** land may be assigned to individuals or groups.

In general, free-running game and unharvested plants are collectively owned. But the work done to reduce the resources into consumable food transforms them into individually or jointly owned property. However, most societies provide for rules for the sharing of food, even when the food itself is privately owned.

Weapons and implements for personal use are usually owned by their creators or users.

CHAPTER 5

CULTURE, SOCIETY
AND THE INDIVIDUAL

5.1   CULTURE AND SOCIETY

The key concept of anthropology is **culture**. It may be defined both

1) **materialistically** (culture is a set of observed behaviors and material objects that help a people adjust to a physical or social environment), and

2) **ideationally** (culture is a set of standards or rules for behaviors and for the making of material objects).

Culture is **learned** from other members of the group; it is not innate.

The concept of culture includes the following factors:

1) the full **range** of behaviors in a group;

2) the **patterns** of behavior (not just the specific actions) which are **typical** of the group;

41

3) the ability to **change** over time as a result of contact with others and interaction with the environment;

4) a set of **symbols** by which the variations in behavior are given meaning;

5) the **social group** in which behaviors are played out;

6) the **rules** defining permissible variations in behavior; and

7) the ability to **transmit** culture from generation to generation.

In summary,

1) every culture represents a limited selection of behavior patterns from the total of human potentialities;

2) this selection is made in accordance with dominant assumptions, which have some survival or adaptive value;

3) every culture is a more or less complete and coherent pattern, structure or system of actions and relationships.

Within a given society, some of the basic postulates of the culture may be known to everyone, while others are known only to certain designated specialists. Some aspects of the culture can be explicitly stated, while others are simply taken for granted. Some aspects of culture represent ideals to which people should strive, while others are statements regarding what people actually do.

The task of the anthropologist is to understand the ways in which elements of a culture (material objects, behaviors, ideas) are integrated into a **functional whole**, rather than to enumerate all the separate parts.

Anthropologists rely on a principle of **cultural relativity** in reaching this understanding. According to this principle, standards of right or wrong are always relative to the culture in which they are found. To attempt to evaluate the behavior of one culture in terms of values of another culture is **ethnocentrism**.

A **society** is a group of individuals united by some common principles (their culture). The society persists through time, although its individual members come and go, to the extent that its defining qualities, and its customary behaviors and ideas continue to be transmitted.

5.2   SOCIAL STRUCTURE AND SOCIAL STATUS

Social structure refers to the patterned ways in which individuals and groups relate to one another within a society. The social structure is composed of

1) social institutions — networks of procedures focused on certain interests (e.g., economic institutions are those centered on production, distribution and consumption);

2) charters of institutions — explanations for why the institutions exist and for what purpose; and

3) social statuses — "job descriptions" for the members of the society. Status can be

   a) ascribed status – the "job" one is born with and cannot change (e.g., "son," "female")

   b) achieved status – the job one learns and assumes as one grows in a society (e.g., "farmer," "husband")

4) social roles — the ways in which the job descriptions are activated in behavior; role is usually described in terms of a permissible range of behaviors, rather than in terms of a specific behavior.

All social structures involve some degree of ranking, since not all statuses are equally valued. But truly hierarchical societies are those in which there tend to be wide disparities in access to wealth and power.

Some determinants of status differentiation are as follows:

1) **Gender** — men and women tend to do different things in all societies; however, *what* they do is culturally dependent, which is why it is better to speak of gender distinctions (a term referring to cultural statuses) rather than sexual ones (a term implying biological aspects).

2) **Age** — in most societies age involves an accumulation of experience, prestige, and sometimes wealth and power; the passage from one age grade to another is often marked by **rites of passage**, rituals by which the society at large recognizes the assumption of a new status; rites of passage are most typically held at birth, puberty, marriage, and death.

3) **Ability** — societies based on merit (achieved status) tend to be individualistic and mobile in their orientation as compared with those based on ascribed status.

5.3 HOW CULTURE CHANGES

A **discovery** results from an awareness of something which has always been around, but not taken into account. An **invention** is an alteration (deliberate or otherwise) in pre-existing materials, conditions or practices so as to form new material or actions.

Invention is relatively rare. Most new things come into a culture by borrowing, or **diffusion**. Material aspects of culture are more readily diffused than are ideas or abstractions. It is rare for something to be borrowed intact. It must usually undergo some reworking in form, use, meaning or function in order to be accepted in new surroundings.

The more two cultures are in contact, the more likely elements will diffuse from one to the other. **Acculturation** is the end result of prolonged culture contact, when one society undergoes dramatic change under the influence of a more dominant society. Culture change may be **voluntary**, by means of trade, alliances, or intermarriage.

It may also be **involuntary**, by means of slavery, conquest, or missionary activity.

Culture may change internally when it is perceived to be no longer in touch with new realities. Such times of **culture crisis** may stimulate a growth of **reactive movements**, such as

1) **Millenarianism** — a movement to raise up a depressed group by means of a special ideology that tells them of their destiny to be greater (e.g., early Christianity).

2) **Nativism** or **Revivalism** — a movement to reconstitute a destroyed but still valued way of life (e.g., the Ghost Dance of the Plains Indians in the late 19th century).

3) **Transitional** — a movement seeking to speed up the acculturation process in order to derive more benefits from the dominant culture (e.g., the Cargo Cults of Melanesia).

4) **Revolutionary** — a movement to overturn the regnant ideology and social system.

5.4   PERSONALITY AND CULTURE

The behavior of individuals is determined, at least in part, by the expectations, rules, standards and norms of the culture of the society of which they are members.

The **personality** of an individual is composed of his or her constitutional characteristics (biological, neurological, etc. factors), physical environment, culture and personal experiences.

Many aspects of a personality are determined during the childhood years, when people are **socialized** (or **enculturated**) — taught the expected rules of behavior in their society. The process of socialization seeks to create adults who are competent to act within the guidelines of their society. Socialization may be carried out by formal means (e.g., in school), or by informal means (e.g., observing older role models).

There have been several important orientations toward the study of personality and culture:

1) Each culture, by emphasizing certain values and behaviors, creates an **ideal personality type**; deviance is always evaluated in relation to that cultural ideal, never to a universal human norm (associated with Ruth Benedict).

2) The repetition of child-rearing practices within a society yields, a **modal personality** composed of the most frequently encountered personality traits in that society; the modal traits taken together are called the **basic personality structure** of that society (associated with Abram Kardiner).

3) The formal aspects of culture (such as family organization) will have a determining relationship to features of child training (associated with John Whiting and Irving Child).

CHAPTER 6

SOCIAL ORGANIZATION

6.1 LIFE CRISES AND TRANSITIONS

All people, in all cultures, must confront four basic life cycle crises: birth, maturity, reproduction, death. Every culture takes note of these critical periods in the lives of individuals, but cultures vary in their emphases on one or more of them, and on the beliefs and activities surrounding them. Rituals commemorating these transitions are known as **rites of passage**.

6.1.1 BIRTH

Many non-Western people are lacking in the scientific information explaining the process of conception, although almost all people recognize the causal association between sexual intercourse and conception in some way. In some cultures, however, such as that of certain Australian aborigines, the link between intercourse and conception is denied: it is believed that the sex act merely opens the womb, although the child is actually the reincarnation of an ancestral spirit who entered the womb.

In most cultures, the prenatal period is marked by magic,

ritual, and taboo designed to ward off evil and protect the un-born baby. Birthing itself, by contrast, is generally treated as a routine act, and is most often handled by older women relatives of the mother, or by a midwife. This is not to say that women in non-Western cultures have a physically easy time in child-birth — simply that the **process** of birthing is treated as an everyday matter.

In most societies, men play a very limited role in childbirth activities. However, men in some cultures practice the cou-vade, a custom by which the father takes to bed and undergoes all the taboos experienced by his pregnant wife; he may also experience "sympathetic" labor pains. It is speculated that the **couvade** is a kind of symbol of the identification of the father with his child. (Keep in mind that in pre-industrial societies, paternity — unlike maternity — is not easily proven, so that other steps may have to be taken to assert the father's role.)

In many societies, the woman and baby remain in seclusion for a period of time, often until a ceremony at which the child is presented to the community and given a name. A child who dies before such a ceremony would be considered a non-person and would not be mourned by the community as a whole.

6.1.2 PUBERTY

Puberty is a universal biological alteration in the condition of an individual, but its social significance varies from culture to culture.

Some cultures treat puberty rather casually, and place no special demands on adolescents; others treat it more seriously and surround it with rituals for one or both the sexes.

1) These rituals may or may not coincide precisely with the

48

onset of biological puberty; they are celebrated whenever the community decides the young person is ready to assume an adult status.

2) Some puberty/initiation rituals are physically very severe, including mutilation of body parts or the undergoing of ordeals (e.g., being sent to survive for a period of time in the wilderness). Initiation rituals emphasize the link between the individual and the community at large — the individual maturation becomes a social act, celebrated and recognized by the group as a whole.

3) Initiation rites also involve the instruction of the new adult in the lore of the culture.

6.1.3 MATURITY

An adult — at whatever age one becomes an adult in a given society — is one who is a full participant in both the responsibilities and the privileges of his or her society. Adulthood is a status usually implying marriage and parenthood, as well as full participation in the economic, religious, and political life of the community, as defined by that culture.

6.1.4 DEATH

Virtually every culture believes in some form of a life after physical death, and so death itself is viewed as another transition, not as an end. However, since the dead belong to a new social category, their relationship to the living may change. In some societies, the dead are benign ancestor figures; in others, they became menacing ghosts to be avoided.

Dead bodies are disposed of in various ways, including burial in the ground, burial in water, cremation, setting away in vaults or other structures, placement on a scaffold for exposure to the elements.

In the case of burial, the body is variously straightened out, or curled up, accompanied by rich grave goods (articles the person had used in life, to accompany him/her in the next life), or unadorned, depending on the culture.

The rites surrounding death have two functions:

1) to commemorate the separation of the spiritual essence from the physical body,

2) to allow for the expression of bereavement among the survivors, and to set the stage for the transfer of property.

6.2   MARRIAGE

No human society permits unrestricted sexual access. All cultures have very definite criteria for establishing a legitimate mating, and set limits on sexual activity outside that legitimate relationship.

Mating is a biological phenomenon: the pairing of individuals of opposite sex for the purpose of sexual relations. Marriage is the culturally sanctioned institution for the regulation of mating.

Marriage is a complex set of beliefs and activities that define and control the relations of the mated pair to each other, to their relatives, their families, and to society at large.

The majority of societies permit, or at least tacitly accept premarital mating. In some cases, premarital sex is seen as a preparation for marriage, not as a substitution for it.

Even when premarital sex is tolerated, marriage itself is rarely left to the choice of the young people themselves. Society has too great a stake in the outcome of marriage to leave it to chance. Society is concerned with the following:

1) the perpetuation of the group in the physical sense,

2) the perpetuation of the culture, and

3) the furtherance of special interests in prestige, property and in the exchange of goods and services between the families of the mated pair.

There are many enumerated rules regulating marriage:

1) Every society has an **incest taboo** — a supernaturally sanctioned prohibition against having sexual relations with certain relatives. But the relatives covered by that prohibition vary from culture to culture. The most nearly universal prohibition is that against parent/child and sibling incest. But many societies extend the prohibition.

   a) In order to understand the extension of the incest taboo in many cultures, it is necessary to understand a basic principle of family organization as studied by anthropologists: in many kinship systems, relatives who stand in different biological relationships to a person may be **classified** (or "lumped") together into a single social category. For example, a man may use the term "sister" not only for his biological siblings, but also for all the daughters of all his mother's sisters. These women, "cousins" to us, are equivalent to one's own sister in certain cultures, and hence tabooed.

   b) The most common form of classification of cousins in-

volves a distinction between **parallel** and **cross cousins**. Parallel cousins are children of siblings of the same
sex; cross cousins are children of siblings of the opposite sex. It is most common for parallel cousins to be
included in the incest taboo, while in many societies,
cross cousins are considered desirable marriage partners. In our kinship system, they are all equivalent —
all cousins — so we must make a special effort to
understand the kinship system of a culture with a different system of classification, lest we makes ethnocentric
judgments about issues of sexuality and marriage. In
fact, cross cousin marriage is a very widespread form,
probably because it serves to promote the interdependence within the society by an ongoing and predictable
exchange of marital partners.

2) **Exogamy** is a social rule requiring people to marry *outside*
the socially designated group to which they belong. The
nuclear family, composed of a married pair and their legitimate offspring, is universally exogamous. But some societies make such larger units as the extended family, the
lineage, the clan, or even the village exogamous as well.

3) **Endogamy** is a social rule requiring marriage *within* a designated social group. Endogamy is much less common than
exogamy. The most famous case of an endogamous social
institution is the **caste** of traditional India. The very rare
cases of parallel cousin marriage are a form of endogamy.
The Biblical Hebrews of the patriarchal period practiced
this form of marriage, which was probably a factor of their
way of life as nomadic pastoral people without central authority, who needed to keep their manpower and herds under a single familial authority. The custom survived among
nomadic Araba until very recent times, but is apparently
dying out as the nomads become urbanized.

4) Some rules serve to encourage marriage among in-laws. Such marriages occur upon the death of a spouse, so as to continue a relationship between the two kin groups of the original marriage partners, and to keep the children of the original union within the extended family. These marriages are known variously as **affinal, substitution,** or **continuation** marriages. There are two basic types:

a) the **levirate**; after the death of a husband, the wife is wed to her husband's brother (or other near male relative).

b) the **sororate**; after the death of a wife, the husband marries her sister (or near female relative).

Modes of Marriage – Anthropologists see marriage in societies other than our own as primarily alliances between two kin groups, not as "love matches" between individuals. There are seven basic ways in which this alliance may be established:

1) **Progeny price** – The family of a young man gives goods to the family of the prospective bride. They are not paying for her, per se (which is why the old term, "bride price" is now seldom used), but rather for the rights over her children. In societies in which the couple moves in with the husband's family, a woman's children belong to that family. The progeny price is a way of compensating her family for the loss of her reproductive facilities on their behalf. In some societies, the husband is considered the legal father of all children born to the woman for whom the price has been paid — regardless of the biological facts of a given case. In most societies, legal paternity is considered far more important than biological fatherhood.

2) **Suitor service** – The prospective groom spends a period of time working for his would-be wife's family.

3) **Gift exchange** – Gifts of equivalent value are exchanged between the families of the bride and groom.

4) **Capture** – Actual cases of abduction of brides is rare, and in no case is it considered to be the social norm. (It is too dangerous and inefficient.) However, in certain cultures, mock abductions are staged. If a young man shows ingenuity and tenacity in carrying out the charade, he is considered worthy of the girl's hand.

5) **Inheritance** – Essentially the same as a levirate or sororate marriage described above.

6) **Elopement** – In some cultures, a couple could succeed in getting married despite social rules by running off together and reaching a designated place of asylum. If they stuck it out there until the birth of a child, they would, by custom, be accepted back into the fold.

7) **Adoption** – A man is adopted into the family of his prospective bride. This situation occurs only when the bride's father has no sons of his own, and needs a male heir. The young man thus ends up marrying his "sister."

Dissolving Marriages — Divorce is always a painful process, but particularly so when the marriage involves considerable exchange of goods and services. The couple is often under great family pressure to preserve the marriage so as not to disturb the ties between the families. However, all cultures allow for the dissolution of marriage, either for very specific causes, or, in a surprisingly large number of cases, by "mutual consent."

6.3   THE FAMILY

When anthropologists study the relationships of marriage and family, they use a shorthand notation system whose symbols allow for the quick diagramming of relationships that would otherwise take extensive narrative description. The following symbols are used in kinship diagramming:

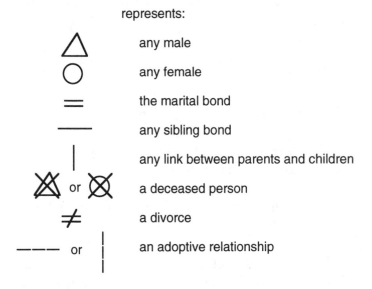

	represents:
△	any male
○	any female
=	the marital bond
——	any sibling bond
|	any link between parents and children
⨂ or ⨂	a deceased person
≠	a divorce
――― or |	an adoptive relationship

All kinship diagrams are drawn from the point of view of a single person at a time. This person, whether a male or a female, is known as **Ego**. Ego is usually shaded or marked in some other way to note his or her special place. All relationships on a kinship diagram are read in relation to Ego. For example,

The woman married to Ego is called a "wife" in our kinship system. She is, of course, also a "mother" to the two children shown on the diagram, and she is probably also somebody else's daughter, sister, or aunt. But in terms of this diagram, we identify her relationship **to Ego** alone.

Marriage establishes the basic unit of family relationship — the **nuclear family**. The nuclear family serves four fundamental functions:

1) to regularize sexual relationships between certain men and women;

2) to bear and nurture new members of the community;

3) to organize and institutionalize a sexual division of labor and to regulate the transfer of property; and

4) to establish the members of the family within a larger network of kin.

Although the role of the family as a social institution has been somewhat de-emphasized in urban, industrial societies, it is still an institution of overwhelming importance.

1) There is no known human society lacking in a family organization.

2) There is no known human society in which the family is not the primary focus of socialization and the model for all later social relationships, no matter how widespread they may become.

Because the family is so basic to every person's social identity, it is the social institution most frequently seen in an ethnocentric light. We must keep in mind that although "the family" is universal, its structure and organization vary widely from culture to culture.

There are two types of nuclear family:

1) That into which a person is born is the **nuclear family of orientation**, in which Ego's statuses are those of child and sibling.

2) That which is established upon marriage is the **nuclear family of procreation**, in which Ego's statuses are those of spouse and parent.

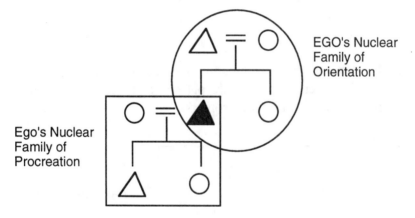

EGO's Nuclear Family of Orientation

Ego's Nuclear Family of Procreation

Our society is quite unusual in its emphasis on the nuclear family. It is much more common for social organization to be based on more extended family groups. One way to extend the family is by extending the marital bond (to create what are called **composite conjugal families**, or **polygamous** unions), which may occur in two ways:

1) **Polygyny**, the simultaneous marriage of one man to two or more women; if the women happen to be sisters, the union is technically called **sororal polygyny**.

57

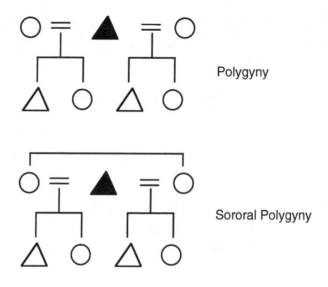

Polygyny

Sororal Polygyny

2) **Polyandry**, the simultaneous marriage of a woman to two or more men; this is a rare pattern, and only occurs when the men in question are brothers.

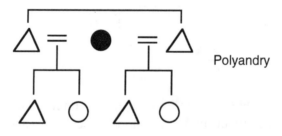

Polyandry

A family in which children, upon marriage, bring their spouses to live in the parental households, such that all their children in turn are raised together, is known as a **joint family**.

All societies $n = 859$	Sub-Saharan Africa $n = 237$	Medi-terranean $n = 96$	East Eurasia $n = 94$	Oceania $n = 126$	North America $n = 218$	South America $n = 88$
69%	82%	80%	82%	62%	58%	41%
17%		2%		17%	24%	40%
14%	12%	18%	11%	20%	18%	19%
	6%		7%			

	Male-focused		Female-focused		Other

Adapted and reprinted from Hoebel, E. Adamson, and Thomas Weaver *Anthropology and the Human Experience*, 5th ed. (1979), page 430. Reprinted by permission of McGraw-Hill, Inc., New York.

FIGURE 6.1 — Relative frequency of male-focused and female-focused residence patterns, according to geographic areas. The male-focused pattern represents viri/patrilocal; the female-focused one, uxori/matrilocal, plus avunculocal.

After marriage, the most important question is where the newly joined couple will live. The decision is rarely allowed to be based on whim. It is, like marriage itself, patterned by rules and expectations:

1) **Virilocal** residence – the couple settles in the vicinity of the husband's kin.

59

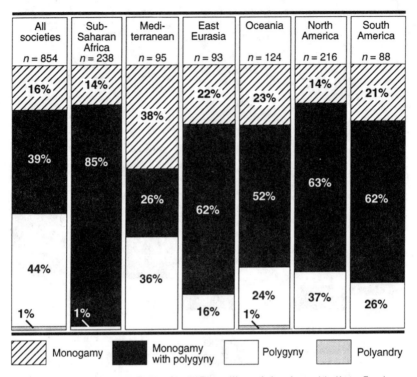

All societies $n = 854$	Sub-Saharan Africa $n = 238$	Medi-terranean $n = 95$	East Eurasia $n = 93$	Oceania $n = 124$	North America $n = 216$	South America $n = 88$
16%	14%	38%	22%	23%	14%	21%
39%	85%	26%	62%	52%	63%	62%
44%		36%		24%	37%	26%
1%	1%		16%	1%		

| | Monogamy | | Monogamy with polygyny | | Polygyny | | Polyandry |

Adapted and reprinted from Hoebel, E. Adamson, and Thomas Weaver *Anthropology and the Human Experience*, 5th ed. (1979), page 431. Reprinted by permission of McGraw-Hill, Inc., New York.

FIGURE 6.2 — Relative frequency of monogamy, monogamy with polygyny, polygyny, and polyandry as expected marriage forms, according to geographic area. (Data adapted from E. Bourguignon and L. Greenbaum, *Diversity and Homogeneity*, table 26, p. 48)

2) **Patrilocal** residence – they settle in the actual household of the husband's father.

3) **Uxorilocal** residence – they settle in the vicinity of the bride's kin.

4) **Matrilocal** residence – they settle in the actual household of the bride's mother.

5) **Ambilocal** residence – they settle in the vicinity of either the husband's or the bride's kin.

6) **Avunculocal** residence – they settle in the household of the groom's mother's brother.

7) **Neolocal** residence – they settle in a new locale, without reference to the location of either family.

6.4   KINSHIP-BASED SOCIAL GROUPS

The family may also be extended through the extension of the lines of descent.

1) A **bilateral** kinship group reckons common descent through both parents (as in our system).

2) A **unilineal** kinship group does so through only one of the parents.

   a) when the line of descent passes through the father, it is known as **patrilineal** descent,

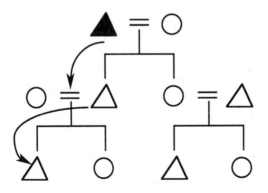

b) when it passes through the mother's line, it is known as **matrilineal** descent; even though it is almost always men inheriting property from other men, in a matrilineal system they will reckon their relationship through their female relations; the typical pattern is for inheritance to pass from a mother's brother to a sister's son.

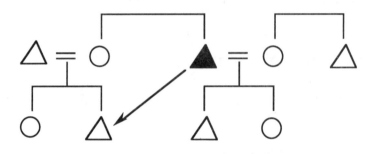

Note that in the above diagram, Ego's property passes to his sister's son, not to his own biological son. The latter will, rather, receive property from his mother's brother.

3) An **ambilineal** kinship group reckons common descent through *either* parental line (but not both, as in a bilateral system).

4) A **double descent** kinship group reckons descent from both parents, but for different purposes; for example, a boy might inherit only material property from his father's side, and only magical powers from his mother's side.

These principles of extended descent create several levels of kin organization:

1) The **kindred** includes all persons to whom one traces a bond, either through "blood" (a **consanguineal** relationship) or marriage (an **affinal** relationship); such persons are known as one's **cognates**. The kindred exists only in societies (such as ours) that practice bilateral descent.

2) The **ramage** includes all persons to whom one is related *either* through the mother or through the father in an ambilineal descent system.

3) The **lineage** includes all persons to whom one is related through the one line prescribed in a unilineal descent system. The vast majority of the world's people live in lineage-based societies. When the lineage is determined by patrilineal descent, the relatives are known as agnatic kin; when it is determined by matrilineal descent, they are the uterine kin.

   A lineage is an extended unilineal kinship group descended from a common, *known* ancestor, going back not more than five or six generations.

4) The **clan**: a group formed when two or more lineages assert a relationship with each other; their common ancestor, however, must have existed so far back in time that he or she is no longer known as a person. Therefore, that ancestor figure is replaced by a mythological figure, often represented by a symbol (such as an animal) known as the clan's **totem**.

5) When two or more clans assert a relationship with each other, the resulting very large groups going back many, many generations in ancestry are known as **moieties** if

there are two of them in a society, and as **phratries** if there are three or more.

The most common functions of unilineal descent groups are

1) to broaden the base of the kinship group through mutual aid, protection, and support in disputes; and

2) to regulate and control marriage.

Other functions of unilineal descent groups are

1) to act as a governing or legal body, regulating disputes and setting or enforcing standards of behavior;

2) to administer common economic property; and

3) to regularize religious observances.

Kinship groups are determined by culture, not by biology. The kinship group represents the culture's fundamental beliefs about how people should behave toward one another. (Keep in mind that in most traditional societies, everyone one encounters is either a relative, or a stranger to be treated with distrust.) In any given kinship system, certain statuses are singled out as being of unique importance; they are given **descriptive** kinship terms — terms that apply to no other category of relative. For example, in our kinship system, mother, father, brother, sister, son, and daughter are all descriptive kin terms because they describe unique relationships. (We may, of course, have more than one brother or sister, but all of them are people who stand in the same unique "biological" or adoptive relationship to us. We may also use the terms "brother" and "sister" to address members of certain religious orders, or to refer to members of one's political party, but these are metaphoric usages outside the kinship system.) This practice emphasizes the special role of the nuclear family in our society.

1) All other terms, however, are formed by lumping people of various relationships together into a single category, and labelling them with **classificatory** terms. In English, for example, **cousin** is a classificatory term because it lumps people of both sexes, of all generations, and people related either through blood or marriage. Such a term is indicative of the social reality that, for most Americans, relatives outside the nuclear family are remote and do not need to be distinguished by special labels.

2) Kinship terms therefore designate categories of social status and suggest expected behaviors linking persons. It is for this reason that anthropologists have spent a great deal of effort in studying systems of **kinship terminology**.

Kinship terminology systems are based on one or more of the following principles:

1) differences in generational level (e.g., father/son),

2) differences in age level within the same generation (e.g., elder brother/younger brother),

3) differences between lineal (those in the direct line of descent) and collateral (those outside the direct line of descent) relations (e.g., father/uncle),

4) differences in sex of relations (e.g., brother/sister),

5) differences in sex of the speaker (e.g., male Ego's brother/ female Ego's brother),

6) differences in sex of the person through whom relationship is established (e.g., father's brother/mother's brother),

7) differences between "blood" relatives and relatives through marriage (e.g., mother/mother-in-law), and

8) differences in status or life condition of the person through whom the relationship is established (e.g., son of a living sister/ son of a deceased sister).

Kinship terminology systems based on classification of parental generation:

1) **Lineal system** – distinguishes lineal from collateral relations (our system) [on the following diagrams, letters stand for kin terms; figures with the same letter would be "lumped" into the same social category]:

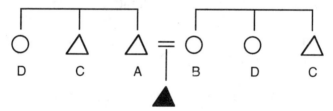

2) **Generational** system – all relatives of the same sex in a given generation are lumped together:

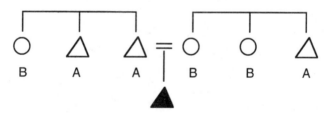

3) **Bifurcate Merging system** – siblings of the same sex are lumped with lineal relatives:

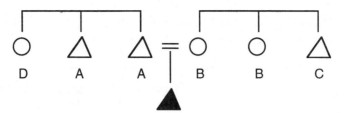

4) **Bifurcate Collateral system** – completely descriptive:

Kinship terminology systems based on classification of cousins:

1) **Eskimo –** related to the lineal; distinguishes lineal from collateral relatives (our system):

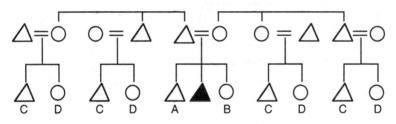

2) **Hawaiian –** related to the generational; all relatives of the same sex are lumped:

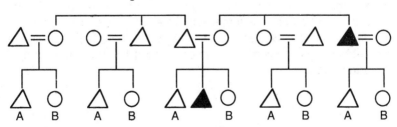

3) **Iroquois** – related to the bifurcate merging; children of
siblings of the same sex are merged with lineal relatives;

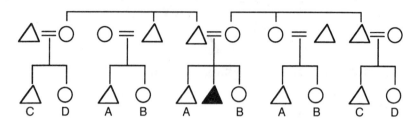

4) **Crow** – found in bifurcate merging systems in matrilineal
descent groups; cross cousins are distinguished from each
other as well as from parallel cousins and siblings; cross
cousins on the father's side are merged with father and
father's sister:

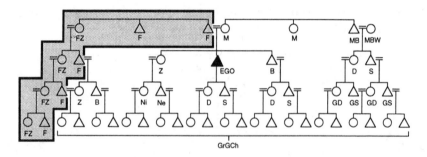

Adapted and reprinted from Hoebel, E. Adamson, and Thomas Weaver *Anthropology and the Human Experience*, 5th ed. (1979), page 430. Reprinted by permission of McGraw-Hill, Inc., New York.

FIGURE 6.3—Crow-type identifications. Note that the male patrilateral cross-cousin may marry ego's mother and is called by the
same term as father. The female patrilateral cross-cousin is merged
with father's sister. Since ego may marry his maternal uncle's wife,
matrilateral cross-cousins are thereby called by the same term as
son and daughter.

5) **Omaha**: the patrilineal mirror image of the Crow; cross cousins are distinguished from each other, as well as from parallel cousins and siblings; cross cousins on the mother's side are merged with mother and mother's brother:

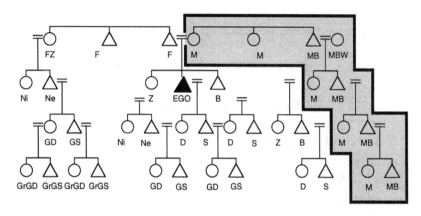

Adapted and reprinted from Hoebel, E. Adamson, and Thomas Weaver *Anthropology and the Human Experience*, 5th ed. (1979), page 431. Reprinted by permission of McGraw-Hill, Inc., New York.

FIGURE 6.4 — Omaha-type kinship identifications. The relatives within the boxed area are members of ego's mother's patrilineage. Females identified as "M" are all classified with "mother" under a term which means "female member of my mother's patrilineage." Note the differentiating terminologies on all generation levels.

6) **Sudanese**: related to the bifurcate collateral; completely descriptive:

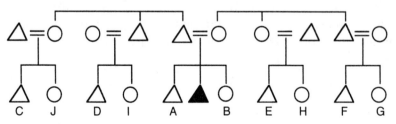

6.5   NON-KIN ASSOCIATIONS AND GROUPS

Non-kin associations often have a recreational factor, but they also serve important economic, political, and ritual functions.

Types of associations include the following:

1) fraternities: perpetuate esoteric lore; maintain order

   a) tribal fraternities: open to all initiated adult men

   b) secret fraternities: open only to selected initiates

2) secular associations: cooperative credit unions; mutual aid societies)

3) military associations

4) age sets: established among people who undergo puberty rites at the same time and who thereafter continue a lifelong association with each other.

Males are more likely than females to form non-kin associations.

Voluntary associations usually complement existing kin groups, but in societies undergoing rapid social and economic change, they may come to replace them. They are associated with increasing size and heterogeneity of the population, and greater division of labor and diversity of interests.

CHAPTER 7

SOCIAL STRATIFICATION AND TRANSACTION

7.1   ECONOMIC ORGANIZATION

Chapter 4 discussed the means by which human beings procure food, clothing and shelter — the basic biological/ecological necessities for life. But goods and services, once produced, must be allocated and distributed. Choices about these matters are culturally, not biologically or ecologically determined, and so **economic institutions** include the following:

1) relationships that promote production,

2) gift exchange, trade, sale, inheritance,

3) normative patterns of use, storage and consumption, and

4) rules of ownership, possession and rights of use.

These factors are aspects of the organization of a society, as discussed in Chapter 6.

Types of consumption include the following:

1) **Primary** – typical of simple economic systems; most goods and services are consumed by the producers and their immediate families or households.

2) **Secondary** – typical of complex economic systems; goods and services are shared or exchanged beyond the primary household unit.

Modes of Exchange include the following:

1) **Reciprocity** – obligatory giving and receiving of goods and services between designated persons or groups.

2) **Redistribution** – some central authority (e.g., a chief, priest, clan leader) receives goods and services as a tribute, and then gives part of them back to the people.

3) **Market Exchange** – direct barter for goods and services, usually via a medium of exchange (i.e., money).

Aspects of inheritance include the following:

1) The three modes of exchange concern exchanges between the living. But in all societies, an important element in the distribution of goods and services concerns the property that passes from the dead to the living. Inheritance regulations are a very important factor in maintaining the continuity of the society.

2) Inheritance is best thought of not as the exchange of specific items of property, but as a transfer of status — the transfer of rights to control property. Transfer of status without inheritance (e.g., election of a new President of the U.S.) is known as **succession**.

3) Patrilineal descent systems operate by the transference from father to son; matrilineal systems involve transfer from mother's brother to sister's son.

4) When siblings (including parallel cousins in some cases) are considered equivalent in social status, there may be **collateral inheritance,** or the inheritance from sibling to sibling, rather than from parents to children. Societies in which this form is practiced tend to favor the continuity of the generational bond based in the nuclear family of orientation, rather than of the lineal principle in the nuclear family of procreation.

5) Incorporeal (non-material) property, such as magical formulas or medical powers, are usually transferred before death, since they involve the possessor teaching something to the inheritor.

6) Husbands and wives rarely inherit from each other in non-Western societies; the property of a deceased spouse reverts to his or her lineage.

In a pre-market economy, goods cannot easily be converted to liquid capital, so property must be inherited by someone who can use it — a man's hunting equipment must be used by another man (e.g., his son), not by his wife.

7) **Testamentary disposition** involves the promulgation of a will (written or oral) to distribute property in the absence of customary norms to designate proper heirs.

8) In order to prevent the dispersion of property (which might occur if there are numerous heirs), some societies have adopted the principle of **primogeniture**, which means that all property passes automatically to the eldest son, who

thereupon assumes the responsibility for supporting the rest of the family. A few societies practice **ultimogeniture**, whereby property devolves on the *youngest* son.

9) In a few societies, social custom mandated the destruction of the deceased's property.

7.2 CLASS, CASTE AND SLAVERY

There are three levels at which inequality among people may be viewed:

1) the biological (people are born with different physical traits and endowments);

2) the individual (people occupy positions of relative prestige within a given institution, such as a clan elder — this situation is known as **ranked status**); and

3) the societal (certain groups of people occupy positions of relative prestige within the society at large — this situation is known as **stratification**).

7.2.1 SOCIAL CLASS

1) A social class is a category of people with a shared social status. Because of their associated roles, they are accorded similar prestige. They share a common lifestyle, and develop common interests. They perceive a common identity that distinguishes them from members of other categories.

2) Types of class systems:

   a) Classless societies – lacking social stratification and distinctions of wealth.

b) Societies with wealth distinctions – prevalence of hereditary slavery; ranked statuses rather than true classes.

c) Dual stratification – two categories of people are recognized, not equivalent to each other, but neither of them in slavery.

d) Elite stratification – emergence of a highly ranked class that maintains its superior position by its control of resources (usually land); simultaneous creation of a propertyless class (proletariat, serfs).

e) Complex stratification – three or more ranked social categories exist, with or without slavery.

3) True class societies emerge with the beginnings of the production of surplus, which is necessary to serve as a marker of differential wealth and access to resources.

7.2.2 CASTE

1) A caste system is essentially a class system from which the possibility of social mobility has been removed.

2) Castes are ranked hierarchically.

3) Caste membership is an ascribed status that normally can never be changed.

4) Castes are usually defined by hereditary occupations, and the inheritance of obligations to provide goods or services to members of other castes. This pattern is known as the **Jajmani** system in India.

5) Interactions between members of different castes are highly formalized, and circumscribed by ritual.

6) **Simple caste systems** (societies with two or three castes):

   a) **Pariah caste** type – members of a hereditary occupational group are treated as low and despicable by the general population.

   b) **Ethnic caste** type – develops when a socially superior, endogamous caste, usually the descendants of conquerors, subordinates another group and bars them from equal privilege.

7) **Complex caste systems** encompass a multitude of castes. The Indian caste system, for example, has hundreds of castes.

7.2.3 SLAVERY

1) In some societies, slaves are **chattels** (treated as non-human, bought and sold like property), while in others, they are considered adopted members of the master's household.

   Chattel slavery usually results from the exploitation of a designated group of people and their systematic degradation. Household slavery may result from more individualized circumstances.

2) Slaves were often the spoils of war, and in some societies, wars would be waged specifically to obtain slaves.

3) Slaves, by definition, were denied citizenship (and its attendant rights and privileges) in the society in which they lived and worked.

7.3 LAW AND SOCIAL CONTROL

All societies uphold normative expectations about proper

behavior, and have the means to enforce those standards. Hence, all societies, by definition, have "law," even if they lack a formal, written legal code or a set of formal judicial institutions.

In order for a society to function, the full potential of human behaviors must be narrowed down to that which is socially tolerable. There must always be a degree of **social control** to guide the individual to conformity with the norms of his or her culture.

Custom consists of sanctioned social norms. Behavior that conforms to those norms is rewarded, and that which deviates is penalized.

1) Sanctions may be **positive** (a smile of approval, the bestowal of privileges) or **negative** (a frown of disapproval, outright ostracism).

2) Sanctions may be **supernatural** (rewards and punishments are thought to be carried out by ghosts, spirits, gods, etc.).

Law is the set of social norms, plus:

1) the legitimized use of economic deprivation or physical coercion,

2) the allocation of official authority (e.g., to police, judges), and

3) the presence of regularity (consistency in the application of the norms).

7.3.1   TYPES OF LAW

1) **Substantive** law – the specific norms to be sanctioned by legal action.

2) **Procedural** (adjective) law – designates the means by which transgressions of the substantive law may be punished.

3) **Organic** law – law that is developed out of the experiences of a people, and reflects their own standards and expectations.

4) **Tyrannic** law – law that is imposed on a people against their will (as through conquest).

7.3.2   FUNCTIONS OF LAW

1) Law defines the obligatory relationships among members of a society,

2) Law allocates authority for the upholding of law.

3) Law disposes of cases as they arise.

4) Law continues to redefine relationships as social conditions change.

7.3.3   CASE (DISPUTE) SETTLEMENT

Case settlements involve

1) presentation of evidence,

2) judicial hearings (presence of a recognized authority to decide the case),

3) supernatural devices:

   a) divination – a seer mystically reveals the truth;

b) conditional curse – a litigant swears, "If I am lying, may the gods strike me down";

c) ordeal – the survivor of an ordeal is held to be innocent; and

d) oath – a formal declaration that the testimony is true.

7.4 POLITICAL ORGANIZATION

Although law can exist without government in the formal sense, the existence of law presupposes some sort of **political process**. The political process, like the law

1) defines behavioral norms,

2) allocates force and authority,

3) settles disputes, and

4) redefines norms for conduct.

But political organization also

1) organizes group efforts at public works (e.g., communal hunts, building a temple),

2) carries out ritual or ceremonial tasks,

3) organizes and maintains the means of economic exchange, and

4) defends the home territory and wages aggression against enemies.

The **state** is a specialized form of political organization. It would be ethnocentric to think that societies without a state-type organization lack political organization.

The state is marked by a defined territory, a population with a common culture, and, most important, a centrally organized government with strong coercive powers.

A political system may be organized using one or more of the following features of the social structure:

1) kinship units,

2) geographic or territorial units, and

3) associational (voluntary groups) units.

Types of political organization:

1) stateless systems — lack formal government covering the entire society; political functions carried out by subgroups; no authority responsible for the society as a whole

   a) undifferentiated systems: small, local, kin-based groups live as autonomous, self-governing units;

   b) segmentary lineage systems: the lineage is the center of organization, although the component segments of the lineage have considerable local autonomy;

   c) age-set systems: political affairs are handled by members of an age-set, which cuts across lineage and village boundaries;

   d) village council: authority is vested in a council or voluntary fraternity; and

e) village or band with headman systems: each local unit has its own formally recognized leaders (as opposed to leaderless, consensus action in [i] above).

2) State systems

   a) chiefdoms – a chief has more authority and prestige than a headman; rule based on delegation of responsibility, rather than on face-to-face social control;

   b) kingdoms – after several generations of a chiefly power passing through inheritance in the same family, the leadership becomes that of a king; development of a formal, hereditary bureaucracy; and

   c) the council – the network of advisors to the leader (a specially chosen group — not everyone in the band, as in a stateless society).

Attributes of politics:

1) it is public, not private (individual or familial),

2) it is oriented toward goals of a public nature, and

3) it allocates and focuses power, and assigns authority for making decisions or directing activities.

Type of organization	Highest level of political integration	Specialization of political officials	Predominant mode of subsistence	Community size and population density	Social different-iation	Major form of distribution
Band	Local group or band	Little or none; informal leadership	Hunting & gathering	Very small communities; very low density	Egalitarian	Mostly reciprocity
Tribe	Sometimes multilocal	Little or none: informal leadership	Extensive (shifting) agri-culture and/or herding	Small communities; low density	Egalitarian	Mostly reciprocity
Chiefdom	Multilocal	Some specialized political officials	Extensive or intensive agri-culture and/or herding	Large communities; medium density	Rank	Reciprocity and redistribution
State	Multilocal, often entire language group	Many specialized political officials	Intensive agriculture & herding	Cities & towns; high density	Class & caste	Mostly market exchange

Adapted and reprinted from Ember, Carol R. and Melvin Ember *Anthropology*, 5th ed. (1988), page 384. Reprinted by permission of Prentice Hall, Inc., Englewood Cliffs, New Jersey.

FIGURE 7.1 — Suggested trends in political organization and other social characteristics.

CHAPTER 8

SYMBOLIC EXPRESSIONS

8.1 CULTURE AND WORLD VIEW

The process of learning the ideas, values, expected behaviors, activities and social structures of one's culture is known as **enculturation** (a term often used synonymously with **socialization**).

Most enculturation takes place during the formative years of early childhood, but in practice it never really stops, as people are constantly being exposed to the cues and models of the people and events among which they live.

When people who have been enculturated in the same way, learning roughly the same things about a culture, they come to share an outlook, which is called the **world view** of that culture.

The world view is a shared perspective on the nature of the world, the people in it and the forces (both natural and supernatural) which help explain it.

The expression of a people's qualitative feelings about the way things are or ought to be is known as their **ethos**.

Most people are unable to give a systematic exposition of their world view and ethos — they take too much of it for granted.

The scientific observer sometimes has a better overall picture of the world view of a culture because he or she perceives it from the outside and is able to objectify and classify that experience. But a world view must be subjectively experienced, as well as objectively documented, because it forms the cognitive, emotional, and spiritual logic that helps us make sense of our surroundings.

Anthropologists thus strive not only to present an objective description of a culture (sometimes called an **etic** perspective on that culture), but also a sense of what that culture means to the people who live within it (sometimes called the **emic** perspective on that culture).

"Etic" derives from the study of **phonetics** in linguistics. Phonetics is the process whereby elements common to all languages are emphasized. It is a way of translating the experience of one language into all others.

"Emic," by contrast, derives from the study of **phonemics** in linguistics. Phonemics is the process whereby linguists try to determine the meaning of units of communication to those who actually use that communication system — regardless of what those units might mean to the users of another communication system.

8.2   RELIGION: BELIEFS AND ACTIONS

Religion is that aspect of a people's world view which deals with beliefs about supernatural, spiritual factors in their world, and with the actions people engage in to deal with that supernatural, spiritual plane of experience.

Anthropologists have long been deeply interested in the phenomenon of religion in comparative and historical perspective.

Early theorists (e.g., Sir Edward Tylor in the 1870s) suggested that religion developed because people needed a way to explain puzzling phenomena in their everyday lives, such as dreams and death.

According to such theorists, the root of all human religion is **animism**, the belief in spiritual beings (which are called in to account for events or circumstances beyond simple logic). "Spirits" are any beings (gods, angels, devils, elves, ghosts, etc.) without flesh and blood, but whose reality is nonetheless unchallenged by believers.

Tylor suggested that primitive people realized that in dreams they went through many vivid experiences that transcended ordinary reality, without the participation of their bodies (which remained inertly asleep). Thus, people came up with the concept of the **soul**, the spiritual part of a person's identity, which could separate from the physical body and engage in transcendent activities outside the body.

The soul came to be thought of as the vital, animating essence of a person.

Death is a form of long sleep. In regular sleep, the person awakes when the soul re-enters the body after its adventures. But in death, the soul does not return to the body.

In Tylor's view, primitive people extended this view to include all living things. Plants and animals, like human beings, have a vital essence – a soul – as well as a material body.

After death, souls may become ghosts, or free spirits. In some cases, they are believed to depart to a distant place, while in other cultures they continue to stay near the places where they lived. In the latter case, they continue to interact with the living, for either good or ill.

Because all living things have souls, Tylor believed that primitive religion took the form of "ancestor worship."

There are also supernatural forces that do not emanate from any specific being. Such a force is called **mana**. It is a supernatural attribute of persons and things, but one which does not derive from their essential identities — they just have it. It gives the person the power to do extraordinary things. For example, in some cultures people with great artistic talent are said to possess **mana**. Or an unusually shaped stone may be said to have **mana** — expressed in terms of curative powers, perhaps. The belief in forces like **mana** is known as **animatism**.

Other theorists derive their inspiration from the French sociologist Emile Durkheim (early part of 20th century), who stated that the public aspects of all religion are of primary importance. If belief in spirits remains only a personal dream, it cannot survive. It is only because belief is communicated and shared that it derives its force. For Durkheim, religion is a **social force** acting to express group solidarity and commitment to a unified social organization, as if to say, "we are all one because we believe and act alike."

For Durkheim, the **participation in ritual** is the essence of religion, not belief per se. Sacred rituals are those which allow people to transcend the everyday (the "profane").

The profane sphere is concerned with naturalistic, objective, rational belief and interpretation. It is characterized by a resigned acceptance of everyday reality.

The sacred sphere is mystical and subjective. It is characterized by the extraordinary, which is approached in an attitude of awe, mystery and caution.

Religion rests on a belief in the supernatural, and develops an ideology and rituals to express that belief.

A widely cited contemporary definition of religion is that of the anthropologist Clifford Geertz. He says that religion is

1) a system of symbols which acts to

2) establish powerful, persuasive, and long-lasting moods and motivations in people by

3) formulating conceptions of a general order of existence and

4) clothing those conceptions with such an aura of factuality that

5) the moods and motivations seem uniquely realistic.

In other words, religion is composed of ideas, objects, norms, beliefs and actions which stand for something that transcends ordinary reality (i.e., they are symbols). These things are put together into an orderly system of thought and action; they become a system of knowledge telling people what the world is like, and what they must do to keep it running properly. These beliefs and actions are communicated in such a way as to create an aura of such powerful reverence and mystery that people are moved to want to believe in and participate in it.

Human beings have apparently always asked *why* things are as they are. **Myths** are sacred stories, drawing on supernatural explanations, to account for the origin of things. Anthropologists are not concerned with the "truth" of a myth — only in the ways in which people recount it, and what it means to their world view.

Myths often deal with the theme of **transformation** — how primal chaos became the ordered world in which people now live. In telling such stories, people can justify the existing order of the universe — and, by extension, of the society in which they live.

In addition to ritual and myth, religion is manifested in beliefs about the ways in which the supernatural must be dealt with. There are two ways in which this is accomplished: religion per se, and **magic**.

"Religion" and "magic" are overlapping spheres of belief and action. The main distinction, in modern anthropological usage, is that in a religious system, the supernatural is believed to be so powerful and transcendent that people are subject to its will, and must deal with it by prayer and supplication. In magic, by contrast, the supernatural is believed to be amenable to control, even manipulation.

The "religious attitude" is one which acknowledges the total superiority of the supernatural powers, and thus adopts a posture of reverence and submission, as manifested in prayer, petition, offerings and sacrifice.

The "magical attitude," by contrast, is one which believes the supernatural power to be controllable under the proper circumstances. If certain spells, incantations, charms or rituals are performed just right, the powers will be compelled to comply.

Magic often seems to be empirically efficacious. It may work by simple coincidence or luck, or it may work through psychological suggestion (people believe so strongly that an expected result will occur that they interpret whatever happens as a positive outcome). Anthropologists are not generally concerned with the "truth" of magic — only in the fact that people believe in it, and with the consequences of their belief in their social lives.

Sorcery is magic turned to antisocial purposes. Magic per se is neither good nor bad — it is only the ends to which it is put that give it a moral coloration.

Sorcery — and "good" magic as well — usually work by the manipulation of ordinary physical objects (bones, potions, clippings of hair) turned to supernatural ends. **Witchcraft** is magic carried out on the purely psychic level. A witch is a practitioner of magic who, unlike other practitioners, does not need to "learn" the lore — it is an innate power (like a kind of **mana**); as a consequence, the witch does not need to deal with physical objects — he or she can deal directly in spiritual forces, again for good or evil. [The familiar image of the Halloween witch in Western culture is obviously irrelevant to this anthropological view of witchcraft.]

Supernatural power is by definition dangerous, and must be approached very cautiously, by those who know what they are doing. As a result, many aspects of dealing with the supernatural are **taboo**.

Taboos are sets of negative sanctions, or statements about behaviors that will cause the supernatural power to harm the incautious user. Tabooed acts (such as entering a place of worship with one's shoes on, or eating forbidden kinds of food) are rarely physically harmful in and of themselves — it is the social consensus that they will be punished by the spirits that make them powerful.

Taboos have three functions:

1) to sustain the awe of the supernatural;

2) to set off the members of one social group from all others (such as the practice of circumcision and the observance of the Sabbath, which helped preserve Jewish identity despite many centuries of exile); and

3) to effect social control.

There are two types of magic:

Sympathetic magic works on the principle that objects that have been in contact with one another will continue to exert a spiritual force on each other (e.g., sticking pins into the stomach of a doll to which has been attached a clipping of the hair of a person, and thus causing that person to experience stomach pains).

Imitative magic works on the principle that mimicking the supernatural effects one wishes to achieve will cause them to happen (e.g., doing a "rain dance" in which the hand and body movements of the dancers pantomimes the falling of the rain).

Although most people in a given society will participate in the ritual observances of the religious/magical system to one degree or another, there are always religious specialists with particular access to supernatural power.

Shamans are practitioners who derive their power directly from a supernatural source, either through a physical experience (e.g., being cured of a life-threatening illness) or a spiritual experience (e.g., seeing a vision). They learn to use the paraphernalia and perform the rites of their system by becoming apprentices to experienced shamans.

There are both male and female shamans, but in any given society, it is a matter of either/or.

Shamans are usually part-time practitioners. They engage in the other activities typical of adults of their sex and social standing, and go into their sacred role only as occasion demands.

Shamans are often people who are marked by some sort of distinctive sign. Such a sign may be something viewed negatively in our culture (e.g., the symptoms of epilepsy, or of schizophrenia, or the practice of transvestism) but which is believed to be a mark of spiritual favor in other cultures. For example, the epileptic seizure is like a kind of highly dramatic sleep — the body appears as if dead, and the mind/soul is literally "elsewhere". The schizophrenic may hear voices or see visions imperceptible to "normal" people, and may thus be thought to be in touch with higher powers. The transvestite (often called a **berdache** in anthropological literature) is a person whose straddles social roles and hence transcends ordinary reality.

Shamans are often very adept practitioners of the healing arts — the setting of bones, delivery of babies, and other medical treatments — as well as more esoteric magical practices. A considerable amount of our modern pharmaceutical array consists of substances extracted from natural sources (plants, minerals) long used by shamans.

Priests are practitioners associated with more complex societies, usually with organized "churches." Because priests are usually full-time specialists, they can only exist in a society with a surplus productive capacity, in order to allow for the support of a "non-productive" class.

Priests rarely have personal spiritual power; they are simply trainees who assume an office. It is the office, not the person, which is vested with supernatural power.

There are three kinds of priests:

1) those who serve at inherited, enduring shrines (or as caretakers of inherited, enduring symbolic paraphernalia),

2) those who serve as family heads in ancestor worship religions, and

3) those who serve cult groups whose interests are directed toward special spirits or deities.

All cultures acknowledge ghosts, but not all believe that these spirits of the dead are of major concern. In those societies in which ghosts are presumed to be malevolent, ghost cults may arise in order to placate the spirits.

Ancestor cults are an elaborated form of the belief in ghosts. They tend to work for the conservation of the society, since they emphasize the continuity of tradition.

Anthropologists no longer believe that the belief in a High God is the end product of religious evolution, an idea common in Tylor's time. The idea of a High God is found not only in the religions of classical antiquity, and in the three modern "religions of the Book" (Judaism, Christianity, and Islam), but in various traditional religions in sub-Saharan Africa — although in the latter the High God is a member of a pantheon of numerous lesser gods, while in the three "universal" religions, the High God is the single, all-powerful deity (**monotheism**).

8.3 LANGUAGE

Language is the most fundamental and most distinctively human attribute because it allows for the transmission of culture.

Most animals can communicate (i.e., exchange information) with each other, but language is more than simple communication. Language is a system of **behavior** encompassing communication. It is based on **oral symbols** which are arbitrary and abstract in nature. The system enables humans to describe, classify and catalog experiences, concepts and objects.

Anthropological linguists are interested in the ways in which language and culture are interrelated.

Anthropologists doing fieldwork in another culture make learning the local language a priority task, since it is difficult to gain a subjective understanding of a culture through translation alone.

Because language cannot be preserved in the fossil record, we can never know exactly when or how it emerged. But we can assume that the growing sophistication of tool-making techniques stimulated a growing sophistication of communication among the early hominids, leading to the development of true human language.

There are no specific organs of speech. The parts of the body we use to make speech (lips, tongue, teeth, etc.) are found in most related animal species, and yet they do not produce speech with them. It is our brain which serves to organize our activity in such a way as to render language possible.

The human brain allows us to structure utterances, impart special significance to them, and use them to express abstract ideas.

Laboratory animals (such as the chimpanzee Washoe or the gorilla Koko) have learned to master certain elements of language. But non-human primates do not do so spontaneously, nor do they, even after training, accord meaning to verbal cues and signs, form them by analogy, and develop a pattern of speech.

Primates in the wild use systems of calls, which are specific verbal cues indicating such things as the presence of food, the presence of danger, etc. But the calls remain discrete entities — they cannot be combined, or changed, or used to express abstract ideas.

Not all human language is speech-centered. We can also convey information by non-verbal cues (e.g., smiling), or by "body language," or by our use of space. The study of "body language" is known as **kinesics**. The study of the use of space is known as **proxemics**.

For example, every culture establishes certain distances for people engaged in communication. Communication within a certain distance is considered "intimate"; that which is more distant is "social," and that which is farthest is "formal" or "public." We are uncomfortable when our sense of distance is violated, because the distance itself is meaningful for us. For example, we are uneasy if a salesperson we hardly know comes into our "intimate" space to convey essentially public information, such as the price of a car. Conversely, we would feel embarrassed if intimate information, such as a marriage proposal, were broadcast over a stadium loudspeaker. These very subtle cues are rarely formally taught; we learn them as we are socialized into the behavioral norms of our culture.

In addition, there are specialized media of communication for special events (e.g., drumming or dancing that "tells a story") or for special circumstances (e.g., the use of American Sign Language by hearing-impaired persons).

But the vast majority of human language in all cultures is carried on through spoken discourse.

Written language is a useful, but by no means necessary or inevitable adjunct to spoken language.

There is no such thing as a "primitive" or an "advanced" language. All languages are adequate to meet the needs of the people who speak them (the principle of **linguistic relativity**).

8.3.1   THE STRUCTURE OF LANGUAGE

Although the content of languages varies widely, all languages may be thought of as code systems; they all operate on the basis of some common operations.

Phonology — The basic elements of all language code systems are discrete sounds. The human "speech organs" are capable of producing a nearly infinite range of sounds. It would clearly be impractical to use all of them in developing a code. So every language selects only a few sounds, which are arbitrarily labelled as meaningful. Native speakers of a language think that these special sounds, called **phonemes**, are obvious and natural, and are surprised when speakers of another language either cannot distinguish them or reproduce them in speech.

No known language requires more than 100 phonemes. Some make do with as few as a dozen; English has 46.

Linguists recognize the phonemes of a language they want to study by the technique of **minimal pairs**. Contrasting sounds that signify a shift in meaning to a native speaker are phonemes in that language. In English, the utterances "cat" and "sat" are alike except for the initial consonants — which thus form a "minimal pair." A native speaker not only hears the difference between "c" and "s," but knows that this shift changes the meanings of the words to which they are attached. We therefore know that "r" and "s" are phonemes in English. By contrast, if we say "pin" and "pʰin" (i.e., add an extra puff of breath to the "p"), we might barely hear a difference, but it doesn't change the meaning of the word. So we know that "p" and "pʰ" are "meaningless" variants (**allophones**) of the same phoneme in English — although the distinction between the two consonants *is* phonemic in certain other languages, such as Hindi.

Morphology — Each language develops its code by putting its phonemes together to form larger utterances. Meaningful utterances, or **morphemes**, are collections of phonemes that have been put together using the rules of combination typical of that language. In English, for example, we do not consider the combination "tl" to be correct, and have difficulty pronouncing it, even though it is a very common form in the native Indian languages of Mexico.

Morphemes that are meaningful in and of themselves (e.g., "boy," "house") are called **unbound morphemes**.

Morphemes that are meaningful only when attached to other ones (e.g., "-es" signifying a plural) are called **bound morphemes**. A bound morpheme is not necessarily a "word" (which is a convention of the written, not the spoken language) even though it is a linguistically meaningful unit.

Syntax — The code continues to build as morphemes are grouped in an order considered correct in a given language. This correct order is known as the syntax of the language. Syntax governs the creation of sentences out of morphemes.

Some languages (e.g., Latin) rely on modifications of the morpheme ("case endings") to convey the relationship of elements to each other. But in other languages, like English, meaning is conveyed almost exclusively by "word order," or syntax. For example, the sentence "Paul loves Mary" may or may not mean the same thing as "Mary loves Paul." The word order suggests, in the former, that Paul is the principal actor, while Mary is the object of his action. But in Latin, "Paulus amat Mariam" means the same thing as "Mariam amat Paulus" because the names have their case endings to indicate the relationship between them; "Paulus" is always the subject of the sentence no matter where in the order it appears.

The overall structural pattern of a language is known as its **grammar**. This structure in and of itself conveys meaning, the study of which is known as **semantics**. The phrase "colorless green ideas sleep furiously" is nonsense on the literal level, and yet because it is grammatically correct, a native speaker of English will recognize its "correctness" even while puzzling over its interpretation.

Although we are born with a genetic capacity to learn language, the content and structure of the language we learn is purely the result of the circumstances of our socialization.

Language can convey social status — dialects within a single language may mark differences in age, gender, socio-economic position, etc.

Differences in language (mutual unintelligibility) are markers of social boundaries, although it must be kept in mind that people may share a common culture, but not a common language (e.g., people in rural French- and German-speaking parts of Switzerland), while in some cases people may share a common language but not the same culture (e.g., native speakers of English in northern Maine and in the Virgin Islands).

Language molds the way speakers conceive of the world around them. It is like a screen through which experience is filtered. For example, the rules of English grammar compel us to structure all discourse in terms of past-present-future orientations; in a language like Hopi, by contrast, "tense" is optional. It is not surprising, therefore, that speakers of English tend to be very concerned with orienting themselves in time, and that they believe "time" to occur in a linear, progressive manner. The Hopi live in a "timeless" world, as compared with ours.

This observation is known as the **Sapir-Whorf Hypothesis**, after the anthropologist Edward Sapir and the linguist Benjamin Lee Whorf, who first suggested it in the 1930s.

The study of how people classify the elements in their world through the language they speak is known as **ethnosemantics**.

The study of the growth and divergence of language is known as **historical linguistics**.

Languages are studied comparatively to determine the de-

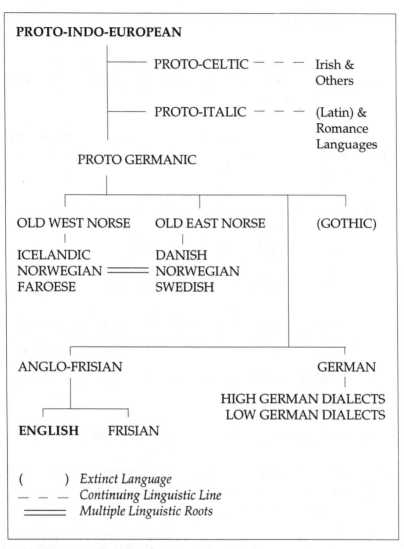

FIGURE 8.1 — Linguistic Roots of English

gree to which they share elements of lexicon (words in usage) and morphology (syntactic structure). **Glottochronology** and **lexicostatistics** are related methods for calculating the length of time two languages have been separated, by measuring the differences in their core vocabularies.

8.4 THE ARTS

"Art" is any activity that serves to enhance the ordinary, to make circumstances more beautiful, or to heighten the pleasure one takes in one's surroundings.

This very broad definition is clearly culturally determined, since standards of "beauty" or "pleasure" will vary from one culture to another.

All art, in whatever culture, involves the following:

1) a specific creator or group of creators;

2) a definite and deliberate process of creation;

3) a definable medium of creation (e.g., paint, stone, words, music);

4) a definite product which is shared with people other than the creator(s);

5) a consensus as to the meaning and value of the product; and

6) a response (formal — as in written criticism — or informal — as in a smile of appreciation) by those with whom the product has been shared.

Anthropologists study art because they are interested in

1) the way in which human creativity is molded by the norms by which people have been enculturated;

2) the ways in which people in different cultures define abstract values such as "beauty," and the ways in which they

learn to express their responses to the presentation of those values; and

3) the ways in which deliberately created symbolic expressions can serve to mold public opinion and express feelings of group solidarity.

In most of the societies studied by anthropologists, art is not a separate category of behavior. Artistic forms of expression are usually thoroughly integrated into other aspects of the culture (e.g., dancing associated with a religious ceremony, a carved ancestor figure to identify a lineage, face or body painting to distinguish among persons of various social classes). The concept of "high art" as an enterprise unto itself seems to be restricted to modern Western culture.

In many societies, art products serve a utilitarian function (e.g., pottery, woven blankets). But when the basic pragmatic purposes of an object are embellished with decorations that give pleasure beyond the utilitarian, the "handicraft" may be said to be a work of art.

All cultures produce art. Art serves a variety of functions:

1) Art serves a **psychological** function. It allows for the expression of feelings and emotions, and it evokes an emotional response in ways that are regularized — tensions can thus be released without threatening the social fabric.

2) Art serves a **societal** function. It symbolically expresses a variety of relationships, beliefs, and institutions, and makes these abstractions meaningful and accessible to everyone. (E.g., not everyone can grasp a highly abstract theological principle, such as the Christian doctrine of the Incarnation, but almost everyone can relate, on some level, to a well made picture of the Madonna and Child which symboli-

cally expresses that doctrine.)

Art may be **naturalistic** (attempting an accurate depiction of "reality") or **abstract**. **Style** is the process of departure from absolute naturalism. There may be a personal style typical of an individual artist, or there may be a style typical of all artists in a given culture or tradition.

Art forms studied by anthropologists may include: painting, carving, sculpture, ceramics, weaving, tattooing, scarification (creating patterns on the skin by raising scars), body ornamentation, dancing, singing, instrumental music and storytelling.

CHAPTER 9

ANTHROPOLOGY AND THE FUTURE

9.1   APPLIED ANTHROPOLOGY

Applied anthropology is the use of anthropological knowledge to contribute to the solution of human problems. Anthropological knowledge about specific culture traits, and about the general processes of social and cultural change is especially important. Anthropology's traditional emphasis on first-hand fieldwork enables anthropologists to contribute an "insider's perspective" when programs are planned for particular communities.

Anthropology has traditionally been a discipline tied to the academic world. The vast majority of professional anthropologists have been employed as university-based teachers or museum curators.

But in the past two decades, a major shift has occurred. At present, the majority of anthropologists receiving advanced degrees are employed outside the academic world. They work in fields such as health care, international development, urban planning and public administration.

Physical anthropologists have been involved in

1) the design of seats in public conveyances,

2) genetic counseling,

3) nutritional counseling,

4) population control/family planning programs, and

5) forensics (e.g., helping police identify human remains).

Anthropological linguists have been involved in

1) understanding the language patterns of people with mental disabilities,

2) bilingual education programs, and

3) programs to preserve Native American languages as markers of Native American social and political identity.

Archaeologists have been involved in government-mandated programs of **cultural resource management** (i.e., the preservation of natural, historic and prehistoric relics, which are frequently threatened by construction and development).

Social and Cultural Anthropologists have been involved in

1) assessment of the *social* impact of development (paralleling the archaeologists' assessment of the impact on material resources);

2) efforts to establish the criteria of membership of Indian

tribes, to help Native American groups qualify for federal assistance;

3) programs designed to make health care outreach efforts more sensitive to the expectations and values of potential client communities (particularly in multi-cultural areas); and

4) evaluations of programs for local, state, regional, federal or international authorities in health care, education or development.

Anthropologists have always had a concern for using their knowledge for the betterment of the human condition, although their ability to do so has been constrained by the political or social demands of the day.

Anthropologists worked in the colonial administrations of the European empires in Africa, Asia, and the Pacific, and in the administration of Indian reservations in North America, and in the overseas trust territories.

During the Great Depression, they became involved in questions of the quality of life in the work-place.

During World War II, they provided information on the cultures of the many parts of the world involved in the conflict.

But the current trend is for anthropologists to build these concerns into full-time careers, rather than keep them as sidelights to their academic careers.

Basic anthropological premises guiding the applications of anthropology to human social problems include the following:

Culture change – Any effort to improve the human condition by definition involves changing culture. Anthropology has a considerable body of empirical data and theoretical studies to describe and explain

1) under which conditions culture remains stable,

2) why it changes,

3) what happens when it changes; and

4) how people react to culture change.

Such information on "natural" culture change is very useful in programs of "directed" or "guided" culture change.

Cultural relativity – Anthropologists can demonstrate that just because people in a given community think or act differently from service providers or policy planners does not mean they are necessarily "wrong" or "backward." Adapting programs of change to be more sensitive to the beliefs and norms of a target community will ease acceptance of such programs.

Culture as adaptation – Human problems (e.g., illness, poverty, illiteracy, etc.) are symptoms of maladaptations to an environment. It is important to understand how proposed changes might enhance adaptation, rather than simply increase the strains of the environment (e.g., introducing a vaccine to reduce the rate of infant mortality without providing means to produce adequate food to feed additional people).

Holism – Applied anthropologists realize that the elements of a culture are interrelated, and that one cannot make a change (even a positive one) in one aspect of a people's life without having an impact (perhaps an unintentionally negative one) on all other aspects of their life.

Applied anthropologists always confront the question: Is change justified?

If so, how can it be achieved with minimum disruption to the culture of the people undergoing change? Ethically speaking, the applied anthropologist may choose

1) not to intervene (the proposed change has too many potential negative outcomes, which even his/her "working within the system" cannot hope to mitigate);

2) to intervene through research (i.e., providing only background information, on the basis of which others will make a judgment about the propriety of intervention); or

3) to intervene actively and provide not only information, but to become an advocate for the interests of the group in question.

When intervention is chosen, the applied anthropologist proceeds through these preliminary tasks, including

1) establishing the goals and terms of the project,

2) entering into a contractual agreement with a sponsoring agency,

3) developing a design (proposal) for research or other action,

4) taking steps to insure the privacy/confidentiality of all information to be gathered;

5) gathering and analyzing data;

6) making recommendations for change based on the data;

7) carrying out the recommendations; and

8) evaluating the impact of the changes.

9.2 THE FUTURE OF SOCIETY AND HUMAN CULTURES

For several million years, human beings lived in small bands that survived by hunting and gathering.

Domestication of plants and animals (ca. 10,000 years ago) enabled people to settle into permanent villages. As population grew, urban centers of trade, government and ritual developed.

Although anthropologists have been most concerned with documenting these vast historical changes, and with describing the processes of culture in living societies that resulted from those changes, they are also interested in the question: where might we, as a species, be heading?

The transformation of the nomadic, pre-literate world into an urban-centered one involved change in the "moral order," which is the set of shared understandings about both individual and common goals. In small-scale, "folk" societies, the moral order is conditioned by the following social factors:

1) the community is small in numbers;

2) interpersonal ties are based on kinship;

3) there are few occupational specialties, and hence few distinctions of wealth and social status;

4) morality is governed by religious/magical views of the nature of the universe; and

5) outsiders are treated with suspicion, or even hostility. These factors are all transformed as civilization develops.

Anomie is the condition resulting from changes that cause the moral order to lose its bonding and motivating force. It is a condition of alienation — a feeling of a lack of identity related to a sense that one no longer has a meaningful role in a meaningfully ordered society. Its main symptoms are apathy and demoralization.

Peasant society is a sub-society of a large, stratified, industrial society. It is characterized by

1) rural residence,

2) familial agriculture (based on privately owned land),

3) mostly subsistence agriculture, with minimal cash-cropping,

4) family-centered social organization,

5) low social status compared with people in the larger urban centers,

6) economic interdependence with and political subservience to the larger urban centers, and

7) attachment to the local community and its traditions.

The expansion of industrial society has meant that the peasant societies (sometimes referred to as "little communities") that began to develop with the Neolithic Revolution have been transformed. Their way of life is becoming absorbed into the larger, global culture.

Even cities are losing their separate identities, as vast areas come to be covered with continuous "urban sprawl" and suburban interconnections.

In order for the "new society" of a continuous, interconnected urban/suburban pattern to survive, it must satisfy the basic prerequisites of all societies. That is, it must

1) maintain the biological functioning of its members (i.e., provide for their basic health and welfare);

2) allow for the reproduction of new members;

3) socialize new members into functioning adults;

4) produce and distribute necessary goods and services,

5) maintain order between individuals and among groups within the society; and

6) define the "meaning of life" and provide a motivation for collective survival.

In a very general sense, it is the task of the applied anthropologist to see that such processes are facilitated even as society expands and transforms itself.

Will human evolution go on forever, or is it possible to reach a point of social equilibrium?

The answer seems to be that if the resources at the disposal of human beings are adequate to meet the needs of the expanded society, then a point of balance between environment and technology may be reached.

The lesson of human evolution is that if technological innovation slows, then social and biological evolution will also slow down.

But if the resources prove to be inadequate, then conflict and competition will continue to be the order of the day, and change will continue as human groups continue to adapt to unstable conditions.

The ESSENTIALS®
of COMPUTER SCIENCE

Each book in the **Computer Science ESSENTIALS** series offers all essential information of the programming language and/or the subject it covers. It includes every important programming style, principle, concept and statement, and is designed to help students in preparing for exams and doing homework. The **Computer Science ESSENTIALS** are excellent supplements to any class text or course of study.

The **Computer Science ESSENTIALS** are complete and concise, with quick access to needed information. They also provide a handy reference source at all times. The **Computer Science ESSENTIALS** are prepared with REA's customary concern for high professional quality and student needs.

Available titles include:

BASIC
C Programming Language
C++ Programming Language
COBOL I
COBOL II
Computer Science I
Computer Science II
Data Structures I
Data Structures II
Discrete Stuctures
PASCAL I
PASCAL II
PL / 1 Programming Language

If you would like more information about any of these books,
complete the coupon below and return it to us or visit your local bookstore.

The ESSENTIALS® of
ACCOUNTING & BUSINESS

Each book in the **Accounting and Business ESSENTIALS** series offers all essential information about the subject it covers. It includes every important principle and concept, and is designed to help students in preparing for exams and doing homework. The **Accounting and Business ESSENTIALS** are excellent supplements to any class text or course study.

The **Accounting and Business ESSENTIALS** are complete and concise, giving the reader ready access to the most critical information in the field. They also make for handy references at all times. The **Accounting and Business ESSENTIALS** are prepared with REA's customary concern for high professional quality and student needs.

Available titles include:

Accounting I & II
Advanced Accounting I & II
Advertising
Auditing
Business Law I & II
Business Management for Profit
Business Statistics I & II
Buying & Selling a Small Business
Corporate Taxation
Cost & Managerial Accounting I & II
Developing New Products & Services

Effective Public Speaking
Financial Management
Income Taxation
Intermediate Accounting I & II
Macroeconomics I & II
Management Consulting
Marketing Principles
Microeconomics
Money & Banking II
Production & Operations Management
Starting Your Own Small Business

The ESSENTIALS®
of HISTORY

REA's **Essentials of History** series offers a new approach to the study of history that is different from what has been available previously. Compared with conventional history outlines, the **Essentials of History** offer far more detail, with fuller explanations and interpretations of historical events and developments. Compared with voluminous historical tomes and textbooks, the **Essentials of History** offer a far more concise, less ponderous overview of each of the periods they cover.

The **Essentials of History** provide quick access to needed information, and will serve as handy reference sources at all times. The **Essentials of History** are prepared with REA's customary concern for high professional quality and student needs.

UNITED STATES HISTORY
1500 to 1789 From Colony to Republic
1789 to 1841 The Developing Nation
1841 to 1877 Westward Expansion & the Civil War
1877 to 1912 Industrialism, Foreign Expansion & the Progressive Era
1912 to 1941 World War I, the Depression & the New Deal
America since 1941: Emergence as a World Power

WORLD HISTORY
Ancient History (4500 BCE to 500 CE)
The Emergence of Western Civilization
Medieval History (500 to 1450 CE)
The Middle Ages

EUROPEAN HISTORY
1450 to 1648 The Renaissance, Reformation & Wars of Religion
1648 to 1789 Bourbon, Baroque & the Enlightenment
1789 to 1848 Revolution & the New European Order
1848 to 1914 Realism & Materialism
1914 to 1935 World War I & Europe in Crisis
Europe since 1935: From World War II to the Demise of Communism

CANADIAN HISTORY
Pre-Colonization to 1867
The Beginning of a Nation
1867 to Present
The Post-Confederate Nation

If you would like more information about any of these books, complete the coupon below and return it to us or visit your local bookstore.

Research & Education Association
61 Ethel Road W., Piscataway, NJ 08854
Phone: (732) 819-8880   **website: www.rea.com**

Please send me more information about your History Essentials® books.

Name _____

Address _____

City _____ State _____ Zip _____

Available at your local bookstore or order directly from us by sending in coupon below.

REA'S
PROBLEM
SOLVERS®

The PROBLEM SOLVERS® are comprehensive supplemental textbooks designed to save time in finding solutions to problems. Each PROBLEM SOLVER® is the first of its kind ever produced in its field. It is the product of a massive effort to illustrate almost any imaginable problem in exceptional depth, detail, and clarity. Each problem is worked out in detail with a step-by-step solution, and the problems are arranged in order of complexity from elementary to advanced. Each book is fully indexed for locating problems rapidly.

Accounting	**Genetics**
Advanced Calculus	**Geometry**
Algebra & Trigonometry	**Linear Algebra**
Automatic Control Systems/Robotics	**Mechanics**
Biology	**Numerical Analysis**
Business, Accounting & Finance	**Operations Research**
Calculus	**Organic Chemistry**
Chemistry	**Physics**
Differential Equations	**Pre-Calculus**
Economics	**Probability**
Electrical Machines	**Psychology**
Electric Circuits	**Statistics**
Electromagnetics	**Technical Design Graphics**
Electronics	**Thermodynamics**
Finite & Discrete Math	**Topology**
Fluid Mechanics/Dynamics	**Transport Phenomena**

If you would like more information about any of these books,
complete the coupon below and return it to us or visit your local bookstore.

Research & Education Association
61 Ethel Road W., Piscataway, NJ 08854
Phone: (732) 819-8880   **website: www.rea.com**

Please send me more information about your Problem Solver® books.

Name _____

Address _____

City _____ State _____ Zip _____

REA's Test Preps
The Best in Test Preparation

- REA "Test Preps" are **far more** comprehensive than any other test preparation series
- Each book contains up to **eight** full-length practice tests based on the most recent exams
- **Every** type of question likely to be given on the exams is included
- Answers are accompanied by **full** and **detailed** explanations

REA publishes over 70 Test Preparation volumes in several series. They include:

Advanced Placement Exams (APs)
Art History
Biology
Calculus AB & BC
Chemistry
Economics
English Language & Composition
English Literature & Composition
European History
French Language
Government & Politics
Latin
Physics B & C
Psychology
Spanish Language
Statistics
United States History
World History

College-Level Examination Program (CLEP)
Analyzing and Interpreting Literature
College Algebra
Freshman College Composition
General Examinations
General Examinations Review
History of the United States I, II
Introduction to Educational Psychology
Human Growth and Development
Introductory Psychology
Introductory Sociology
Principles of Management
Principles of Marketing
Spanish
Western Civilization I, II

SAT Subject Tests
Biology E/M
Chemistry
French
German
Literature
Mathematics Level 1, 2
Physics
Spanish
United States History

Graduate Record Exams (GREs)
Biology
Chemistry
Computer Science
General
Literature in English
Mathematics
Physics
Psychology

ACT - ACT Assessment

ASVAB - Armed Services Vocational Aptitude Battery

CBEST - California Basic Educational Skills Test

CDL - Commercial Driver License Exam

CLAST - College Level Academic Skills Test

COOP & HSPT - Catholic High School Admission Tests

ELM - California State University Entry Level Mathematics Exam

FE (EIT) - Fundamentals of Engineering Exams - For Both AM & PM Exams

FTCE - Florida Teacher Certification Examinations

GED - (U.S. Edition)

GMAT - Graduate Management Admission Test

LSAT - Law School Admission Test

MAT - Miller Analogies Test

MCAT - Medical College Admission Test

MTEL - Massachusetts Tests for Educator Licensure

NJ HSPA - New Jersey High School Proficiency Assessment

NYSTCE - New York State Teacher Certification Examinations

PRAXIS PLT - Principles of Learning & Teaching Tests

PRAXIS PPST - Pre-Professional Skills Tests

PSAT/NMSQT

SAT

TExES - Texas Examinations of Educator Standards

THEA - Texas Higher Education Assessment

TOEFL - Test of English as a Foreign Language

TOEIC - Test of English for International Communication

USMLE Steps 1,2,3 - U.S. Medical Licensing Exams

If you would like more information about any of these books,
complete the coupon below and return it to us or visit your local bookstore.

Research & Education Association
61 Ethel Road W., Piscataway, NJ 08854
Phone: (732) 819-8880   **website: www.rea.com**

Please send me more information about your Test Prep books.

Name_____

Address_____

City_____ State _____ Zip _____